PENGUIN BUSINESS

EMOTIONAL INTELLIGENCE

Rajagopalan Purushothaman, popularly known as 'Puru', is an alumnus of Institute of Management Technology, Ghaziabad, and one of the leading learning and development and organizational development professionals in India with diverse experience spanning four decades in telecom, retail, manufacturing, consulting and services businesses.

Puru specializes in setting up corporate academies for large corporations such as the Reliance group, which includes Reliance Retail and Jio. He played a pivotal role in both the retail and telecom revolutions in India by establishing fourteen academies to help businesses succeed. The academies have directly impacted the lives of more than one million human resources.

He has facilitated more than 1000 workshop for senior level executives on leadership and personal effectiveness. He is credited with designing and implementing business-impacting learning solutions across twenty-eight organizations.

A winner of the Brandon Hall Award, the Asian Human Capital Award (Singapore) and TISS-Leapvault Award, Puru serves as chief mentor to AssessHub and is a member on the advisory board of Cheers Interactive.

PRAISE FOR THE BOOK

'The world today is exponentially being transformed by digital technologies, and the crisis has accelerated this transformation. Puru's book helps us to understand how we can reach escape velocity by focusing on being human and tapping into our emotional intelligence (EI). He guides us through practical, easy-to-remember exercises to intentionally focus on our emotional quotient. The five components of EI—self-awareness, self-regulation, self-motivation, social skills and empathy—are critical for leaders to take care of people during the crisis and accelerate business recovery and growth'—**Mamatha Chamarthi, chief digital officer, software business growth officer and CEO of software business, Goodyear**

'*Emotional Intelligence*—Puru's book is the need of the hour! Puru has excellently defined self-awareness and self-regulation in his book. The narration of emotions and feelings is articulated so beautifully that right from a schoolboy to a scholar can read and can understand. The language is so simple yet so powerful, which is the essence of El. The example he highlighted about Sandeep reminds me of the cortisol effect, when aggression jeopardizes the development of today's younger generation and, especially, of corporate executives. The chapter on self-motivation is my favourite in the book as Puru has beautifully articulated the evidence of self-motivation, which can be practised by all and not necessarily only corporate professionals. Puru has given us the perspective in excelling emotional intelligence with wider possibilities, it's now our choice'—**P.K.C. Bose, co-founder, ENREGO Energy GmbH**

'Importance of an emotionally intelligent leader is experienced both in peaceful and turbulent times. In pandemic (e.g., COVID-19) situations, the EI capabilities help in navigating the uncertainty and potential loss surrounding the pandemic. Leaders with EI have awareness, perception, composure and exceptional self-control, which enable them to develop and propel the firm and society's path of success through empathy, influence and collaboration. The best part of EI is that it is a learnable skill. Rajagopalan Purushothaman's book on EI has been well crafted to develop the EI skill sets in an individual. A firm can use the frameworks and processes provided in the book to cultivate leadership skills in its workforce. The book is amazingly simple to read with a high impact. A must-buy for both industry and academicians'—**Prashant Salwan, professor of strategy and chairman, Executive Education, IIM Indore**

emotional intelligence

MASTERING PERSONAL AND PROFESSIONAL GROWTH IN THE DIGITAL ERA

RAJAGOPALAN PURUSHOTHAMAN

**PENGUIN
BUSINESS**

An imprint of Penguin Random House

PENGUIN BUSINESS

USA | Canada | UK | Ireland | Australia
New Zealand | India | South Africa | China | Singapore

Penguin Business is an imprint of the Penguin Random House group of companies
whose addresses can be found at global.penguinrandomhouse.com

Published by Penguin Random House India Pvt. Ltd
4th Floor, Capital Tower 1, MG Road,
Gurugram 122 002, Haryana, India

First published by SAGE Publications India Pvt Ltd. 2021
This edition published in Penguin Business by Penguin Random House India 2024

Copyright © Rajagopalan Purushothaman 2021

ISBN 9780143464150

Typeset in 9/13.5 pt Georgia by AG Infographics, Delhi.

Printed at Repro India Limited

www.penguin.co.in

Dedication

To all the people who wish to be more emotionally intelligent.

Dedicated to my late father K. Rajagopalan and mother Saroja Rajagopalan and my granddaughter Kiara and my grandson Leon.

Sanskrit Sloka: *Yam hi na vyathayanthyethe purusham purusharshabha Samadhukha sukham dheeram somruthathvaya kalpathe.*

It personifies emotional intelligence and states that 'a person who is calm and remains unperturbed by either pain or pleasure is the one who attains immortality.'

The great philosopher Aristotle summed up emotional intelligence by stating, 'But to be angry with the right person, to the right degree, at the right time, for the right purpose and in the right way—that is not easy.'

Contents

Foreword

The world is becoming increasingly VUCA (volatile, uncertain, complex and ambiguous). Emotional intelligence (EI) constitutes a set of skills that are critical for steering our path through the complex by-lanes of modern living. Surprises await us at every corner. We need to understand our emotional responses to external stimuli (self-awareness), know how to control our responses (self-regulation) and keep motivating ourselves to stick to the path of our chosen goals (self-motivation). Since man is a social animal, empathy (understanding others) and social skills are equally important for success in the modern world. All of these five components are elaborately covered in the book.

The five components come alive for the reader of the book through a large number of cases and examples from daily lives with which any reader will readily identify. I have maintained that a good guru is one who can not only simplify a complex concept for the *shishya* but also enable him to embed learning in such a way that it becomes useful to the *shishya* throughout his life. Puru is an extraordinary guru who has used examples from his own life and extensive corporate experience to illustrate his book. He has used all his vast experience as a learning professional to design a variety of exercises to ingrain learning and to develop habits that will enable the reader to apply the same in his/her own life whenever appropriate.

I would like to share my own experience with the reader. Puru sent me the manuscript of this book and requested me to write a foreword. Given the size of the book, I budgeted for a week or around 20 hours to do justice to the task. However, as I started reading, I found that I was forced to pause after each case/example and relate it to my own past experience. I must add that my own mental models were substantially enhanced and, in many cases, modified as I reflected on these cases. I realized that I was taking more time than I had bargained for. I was, however, getting far higher value than a cursory reading and understanding of the content would ever have given me.

Since it may help other readers, I recommend the following habits that I have tried to adopt for continued learning after reading Puru's book *Emotional Intelligence*.

1. I spend a few minutes before sleep every day introspecting the key incidents of the day in many of which I, too, played a part. I think of the emotions and thoughts of the key players and reflect on how I could have been more effective.
2. When I watch a movie, read a book or even newspaper stories, I have started to think about the thoughts, emotions and experiences of the key players.

The aforementioned exercises help me build my own storehouse of life experiences, which hopefully will help me to steer my path wisely when confronting similar situations in the future.

Thank you, Puru, for a very useful and timely book on an important subject. I hope that other readers of your book will find it equally useful.

—**P. Raghavendran,**
President, Reliance Industries Limited

Acknowledgements

The support and encouragement received from the following persons made it possible for me to complete this book.

My mother Saroja Rajagopalan, for being an exemplary living example of a person leading an emotionally intelligent life.

My father, Late K. Rajagopalan, for being the inspiration to pen down a book and equipping me with communication skills.

My wife Priya and my daughters Pavitra, Prarthana and son-in-law David Liaño González for their constant encouragement and feedback.

Sudha Venkatesh for offering to edit the book.

Arnab Guha for painstakingly editing and offering good suggestions.

And numerous other friends who encouraged me to write a book.

Introduction

The 20th century witnessed an unprecedented industrial revolution that changed the way the human race thought, lived, behaved and acted. The social fabric underwent a dramatic change as we migrated from the agrarian economy to the industrial economy. That compelled the mass migration of workforce from the rural hinterland, leading to the creation of megacities that we witness (live in/see) today. This seismic shift changed the entire social structure, leading to the breakdown of the joint family system prevalent in the agricultural era into nuclear families. It moved from community-centric to family-specific behaviours and practices. The industrial workforce had to spend several hours together within the walls of the factories. The competencies related to working together as a team, managing conflicts and building interpersonal skills gained importance. The organized industrial workforce was needed to be managed effectively to achieve high levels of productivity. The information era that caught up three decades ago brought in the need to develop skills in people to effectively deliver services. This era focused on managing the expectations, the appetite for growth and other aspirations of the workforce.

We are at the threshold of the next biggest change in the form of industry 4.0—the digital era. Technology is the key to enable this revolution wherein the routine and repetitive will be replaced by technological solutions. The human race has repeatedly proven its ability to adapt to changes in the environment and societal structure. The next industrial revolution would change the way we work, live and interact with people and, hence, would bring along a new set of challenges. The most significant challenge would be our ability to deal with others. Technology would ironically create more space between people in this overcrowded world.

The social system that enabled us to master the skills in the earlier industrial revolution is likely to change drastically. Dependence on the family system to build up some of the skills would be weakened. The family system is at a risk, due to either lack of time or people's need for independence. How would the next few generations acquire the necessary survival skills?

In this context, EI has gained significant importance. The ability to manage emotions in a complex, fast-changing and uncertain world is likely to be a significant challenge for the next generation. No effort is too small in building EI competencies in people to navigate through the next industrial revolution. The goal of creating emotionally intelligent future generations can be achieved by leveraging all types of learning platforms apart from the formal education system. The relevance of the content of our current education system would be severely challenged and likely to undergo a sea change. Countries that fail to adapt and change their education system would be left behind in this critical industrial war. The course content, methodology and delivery mechanism for building skills would be under the scanner and is likely to experience a welcome change. The learning ecosystem in organizations and independent learning platforms will fill the void created by the formal education system.

1

Explaining Emotional Intelligence

The world around us is undergoing changes at a fast pace. The social fabric and value system are constantly adapting to emerging dynamics. The rate of change witnessed in the current century is unprecedented in the history of mankind, and the advent of technology is changing our lifestyle significantly. This has brought distinct benefits such as better quality of life, enhanced comfort, productivity, convenience and efficiency. From an era of scarcity, we are moving towards abundance. Access to information and education has been revolutionized. There is no doubt that we need to celebrate the path-breaking achievements of human intelligence.

In the bargain, we have also invited several challenges. These changes are irrefutably impacting our physical and mental health, relationships, stress levels and societal structure and values. The turmoil of this change has impacted people across countries, communities, families and at the individual level. In fact, this change stems from individual effectiveness. Some of the consequences of these changes are as follows:

- High level of competition
- Depression and anxiety
- Lack of self-esteem

- Work-life balance
- Break in relationships
- Restlessness
- Need for instant gratification
- Individualism

The aforementioned consequences are manifested in our lives as various incidents such as:

- Stress-related diseases such as heart ailments, anxiety and depression
- Lifestyle issues such as diabetes, insomnia and indigestion
- Early physical maturity
- Single parenthood
- Late marriages and early divorces
- Mindless entertainment and shopping
- Addictions to substances and unhealthy food
- Lack of meaning in life and spiritual vacuum
- Compulsion to look good physically

Technology and Human Emotions

Human emotions are precious, but they can be self-destructive if not managed well. Unregulated emotions in the absence of emotional intelligence (EI) can lead to ineffectiveness. The field of EI has gained a lot of significance lately, fuelled by the onslaught of technology and also by the way people interact with each other.

In this ever-changing modern world, a significant part of human interactions is likely to be with machines, thanks to the phenomenal technological innovation in areas such as artificial intelligence, machine learning, robotics, 3D printing and nanotechnology. Humans are likely to lose touch with how to effectively interact with each other. We have already begun to see symptoms of personal disconnection in our families and in our workplaces.

Today, we all prefer to spend more time with gadgets and machines rather than with people around us. Linda Stone, a technology writer and consultant, coined the phrase 'constant partial stupidity' (CPA), which is a worrying syndrome that has caught up with millennials. Our attention span is limited to a particular task and our focus keeps shifting. This can result in a stressful lifestyle, as the mind is continuously wandering across various stimulus from the environment, leading to attention span deficit.

According to a research paper published in the *Harvard Business Review* by Dr Matthew Killingsworth, author of the article 'A Wandering Mind Is an Unhappy Mind', constant mind-wandering is the highest contributing factor towards unhappiness. The opposite of CPA is focus that can be developed with the help of EI. Major contributing factors for CPA include social media, remote control devices, a vast array of digital games across age groups and an abundance of media content streaming online from all over the world.

The irony is that digital space is leading us on the path of great progress and, sadly, also towards personal isolation in this crowded world. The time invested by our earlier generations in meaningful interactions with people, building intimacy and strong relationships, is being hijacked today by predatory social media. Our bond is more tilted towards devices rather than towards people.

Recognition gained in social media is impersonal and is often mistaken for true love, affection and intimacy. Several thousands of hours in a year are consumed in this manner, leaving us hardly any time to connect with people in flesh and blood. Conventional wisdom, which claims that man is a social animal, is likely to be severely tested in the near future. The digital world encourages us to spend time alone. It rather isolates us from reality, and we tend to live in a make-believe world.

Recent experience during the COVID-19 pandemic, which shook the world and changed our lifestyles drastically, offered us significant messages. Families living under one roof were locked up in their chambers of the virtual world. It was reported that the divorce rate in China shot up significantly, as couples were spending more time with each other during the quarantine period. Sadly, due to the habit of escaping to the virtual world, couples today are struggling to adapt to each other. Thanks to technology, we are connected globally like never before, yet, ironically, there is a glaring disconnect with people close to us.

It's yet a bridge too far for machines to lend a personal touch and offer socially intelligent emotions such as love, care, comfort and empathy. The human mind has evolved wonderfully. It is capable of questioning, of delving deep within to find the meaning and purpose of life. It is capable of deciphering the vast universe in its quest for the ultimate truth. It would be criminal to let such a wonderful entity wander and move towards a self-destructive mode. Machines may well take their own time to read human emotions and act with EI.

Future Competencies in Industry 4.0—The Digital Era

In the future digital era, the significance of EI will gain further importance as technology such as artificial intelligence and automation are poised to partly or fully replace human intervention. Humans will be valued for their unique characteristics and skills in the digital world. The World Economic Forum indicates, 'Skills on-demand beyond 2020 would be complex problem-solving, critical thinking, creativity, people management, coordinating with others, emotional intelligence, judgement and decision-making, service orientation, negotiation and cognitive flexibility.' It specifies EI as one of the many vital competencies. According to Edward D. Hess, author of the book *Learn or Die*, it is highly unlikely that we would be able to automate social and EI in the near future. The differentiator in the war for talent would be persuasion and EI, as compared to technical skills.

It is interesting to note that many of the other skills highlighted earlier stem from EI. There is no doubt that EI is going to be one of the differentiating competencies in Industry 4.0. The digital era welcomes us, provided that we are equipped with the required skills. Failing to adapt to futuristic competencies will ensure that we are left behind. Our education system, therefore, has to keep pace with these emerging dynamics.

If the current focus on cognitive skills is sustained, we might have a future workforce with the necessary knowledge, but without the ability to apply the same in real-life situations. They would be unable to work with people and get things done. If academic institutions fail to equip students with these skills, learning platforms would attempt to bridge this gap.

We witness examples of globally recognized and successful entrepreneurs with a high IQ and are short-tempered. Just imagine the scenario wherein the entire senior management team of the organization has similar traits. It would pose a major challenge, as retaining talent would be a Himalayan task. At times, such damaging traits displayed by the entrepreneurs are compensated by the people around them who do the balancing act.

An interesting research was conducted by Dr Cary Cherniss, Rutgers University, on the impact of EI on business outcomes in 19 different businesses and role holders. The study was done on recruiters for the US Army, partners in consulting firms, top-level executives in organizations, sales clerks, mechanics, sales agents, insurance agents, supervisors of manufacturing plants, retail chain store managers, financial advisors and debt collectors. Empirical data established the positive impact of EI on top-line, bottom-line, business results, revenue, conversion rate and other business parameters. Often, these softer aspects are difficult to measure and hence ignored at the peril of the business outcome. Recruitment based on EI would help to choose the right candidate and investing in EI training will provide hard business results.

A significant part of training for medical doctors includes 'bedside manners' that emphasize interactions with patients. It includes restoring confidence, providing comfort, managing tone, body language and suppressing negative facial expressions to reduce fear and anxiety in patients. Medical professionals need a significant level of EI training to deal with pain, anxiety and fear in patients. EI plays a significant role in the journey towards becoming a successful medical practitioner.

The city of Kota, the ultimate destination for IIT aspirants, witnessed 72 suicides between 2011 and 2015. The cause was stress and anxiety experienced by these students during their preparation for the coveted examination. The major reason for this was their inability to manage their emotions under stressful situations. In fact, some of the IITs run the 'Centre of Excellence for the Science of Happiness'. The irony is that students with the highest IQ are not capable of understanding and managing their emotions.

In Pursuit of Happiness

The Government of Bhutan developed the 'gross national happiness' (GNH) index as the country's measure of success in place of the conventional GDP. Psychological well-being, good health, a meaningful use of time are some of the parameters of GNH measurement. It was developed in the late 1970s and has been growing in popularity of late.

The first World Happiness Report compiled at Columbia University resonated this idea of being an ideal measurement of the health of a country rather than being confined to a measurement of economic activity.

What is the purpose of financial well-being and prosperity in the absence of happiness?

Emotional well-being holds the top spot in the measure of GNH. Happiness at an individual level is indispensable for achieving national-level happiness index. In other words, managing emotions plays a significant role in promoting happiness in humans.

I had the privilege and opportunity to climb Mount Kilimanjaro under the able guidance of my son-in-law David Liaño González, in the joyful company of my daughter Prarthana. David is an international athlete with diverse interests in climbing, paragliding, running, travelling and adventure. It is no surprise that he found a rightful place in the Guinness Book of World Records for being the first mountaineer to double summit the Mount Everest from both Nepal and Tibet.

Walking the steps across the Kilimanjaro mountain range with David and Prarthana offered me some of the best lessons of my life in managing emotions. Being constantly aware of my body and mind was the first significant learning. The ability to understand and listen to one's self (self-awareness) and the ability to get rid of disruptive feelings when faced with odds (self-regulation) are valuable life traits that I was fortunate to experience. I also gained the thought to not give up when faced with challenging situations, unless it is a medical exigency (self-motivation). What I learnt in this eye-opening summit would stay with me all my life. I did face a severe challenge, just 200 m before the summit. The lack of oxygen and the strong crosswinds took a toll on me, and I had to pause my ascent. My learning however continues.

Emotional Memory

Take a few seconds and think of the most memorable moment in your life. It is very likely that we would quickly recall an emotional moment that we experienced. Emotionally charged moments could be the birth of a child, a well-deserved recognition, meeting your life partner, a notable achievement by your child, the first earnings of your life, a promotion that you gained, etc. Emotional responses are strong and are etched in our memories for a long time. These strong drivers play a major role in every day of our lives. Every action that we take is driven by a physiological or emotional need. Once we recollect memorable moments, we might struggle to remember events and activities from the day before or the day after a memorable event. But the emotional memory related to the occasion is still freshly alive. Emotions influence our behaviour and, hence, we must learn to manage them effectively for our overall well-being.

Competencies Influenced by EI

EI is about dealing with emotions in self and others, effectively leading to better interpersonal skills, conflict management, teamwork, relationship building and understanding. EI influences a whole lot of human competencies, which in turn influences the effectiveness of both our personal and professional lives. It is indeed a powerful gateway to wholesome effectiveness in all realms of life. The importance of EI is further amplified by the fact that it has a far-reaching influence on the way we lead our lives. It is our perennial insurance towards lifelong effectiveness.

Challenges in Formal Education System

I had the opportunity to closely observe the case of a CEO of a large organization. He was brilliant in his job and was a domain expert, with a deep understanding of the business. He was a smart strategist and often came up with effective business-related ideas and solutions. He was good with numbers and had an astute memory. After a tenure of two years, he was recalled from the position of a CEO. All the senior team members reporting to him, without an exception, were unhappy with him. The common complaint was that he had scant respect for other's opinion. He was aggressive and often insulted his team members. His team members took up the issue with the higher management. He was counselled on a couple of occasions, but it had little or no impact on his style of working. He firmly believed that there was nothing wrong in the way he was functioning. He ultimately paid the price when he was shunted out of the assignment. Managing people effectively is possible only with EI, as IQ by itself provides little help.

The formal education system is attempting to mass-produce skill sets for blue- and white-collar jobs. The focus is more on succeeding in formal entrance examinations, not on developing life skills. A major change in the system, challenging the status quo, is not far away. The differentiating factor between success and failure in the current education system is based predominantly on logical and mathematical intelligence, a test of memory and vocabulary.

The vacuum in the system is especially evident in certain basic human competencies, such as managing conflicts, leadership skills, relationship-building capabilities, collaboration, working in teams, interpersonal skills, understanding people and adaptability. The current system fails to address any of these important human competencies that truly determine success and failure in all walks of life.

Overemphasis on developing IQ has produced the desired results, as is evident from the high scores obtained by students in their academic tenure. However, EI is dropping over the years, the evidence of which can be seen in the rise in aggressive and unruly behaviour, impatience, attention deficit, inability to take failures and the need for instant fulfilment of wants. What is not cultivated cannot be harvested. The seeds of EI has to be sown at an early age so that one can reap its benefits at later stages of life. The time is not far away when EI would be an integral part of our education system.

Conventional intelligence being IQ, when backed with a good supply of EI, can be termed as as 'emotigence'. Possessing a few lopsided intelligences would no longer be a potent weapon for achieving success in the future unless it is clubbed with a good amount of ability to manage our emotions. 'Excelligence' is another expression we can use to explain the idea that when multiple intelligence are merged with EI, it fuels the intelligence to excel in multiple walks of life.

EI Learnability

Building and driving EI is very much possible with concerted effort. It is important to understand with clarity the significance of why, what and how to develop EI. By understanding why and what of EI, we gain the conviction and resolve to develop it. Unlike IQ, which tends to show marginal improvement after the age of 18–20 years, the development of EI is not constrained by age. In fact, IQ is likely to drop as we grow older, due to lifestyle and stress. EI does gradually get better with age-related life experiences. Through EI training, we can fasten the process and reap the benefits for a larger part of our lives.

EI and Parenting

Kaniyan Pungundranar, an ancient Tamil philosopher from the Sangam age 3,000 years ago, described in his writings as follows:

> Where there is righteousness in the heart, there is beauty in the character, when there is beauty in the character, there is harmony in the home, when there is harmony in the home, there is an order in the nation, when there is order in the nation, there is peace in the world.

This was ably narrated by Late Dr Abdul Kalam, the former president of India, in his speech at the European parliament. This astounding thought summarizes the importance of achieving harmony and happiness in our homes through right parenting.

The initial seed of EI starts with parenting. It is one of the most challenging and important tasks in our lives. The irony is that most parents today are not equipped to do justice in nurturing the child as they themselves are not formally trained in this subject. The experience of bringing up a child is a matter of self-learning through trial and error. There is no doubt that a happy family environment creates the ideal condition for the child to develop a strong foundation of EI capabilities. It is needless to mention that parents with higher EI would be able to percolate this intelligence to the next generation.

In the formative ages, children majorly learn from the behaviour demonstrated by their parents at home. It goes without saying that ineffective behaviour should be avoided or minimized in the family environment in which the child is brought up. The set of negative behaviour, which is unconducive for the effective development of EI, includes assault, violence, rape, stealing, lying, killing, destruction of property, aggressive behaviour, ill-temper, nagging, addiction, depression, pessimism, jealousy, frigidity, intolerance, stubborn demeanour, inflexibility, overindulgence, tendency to exploit, restlessness, stress and avoiding responsibilities.

The set of positive behaviours that sow the seeds of stronger EI includes acknowledgement, acceptance, admiration when due, appreciation, approval, seeing as competent, encouragement, liked and listened to, showing importance, loved, seen to be in control, radiating strength, recognized, respected, feeling safe, supported, trusted, understood and valued.

All of the emotional needs met and not met, have a strong impact on the child during the nurturing stage. By recognizing and validating the thoughts and feelings of our children, we teach them to trust their instincts. Lesser the unmet needs, the more emotionally healthy the child would be.

When prospective parents meet each other, both might have certain unmet needs that affect their own self-esteem. Parents with high self-esteem tend to experience a healthier relationship that in turn influences the EI of the children in the family.

Negative and positive feelings affect the child, even during pregnancy. Fear, anxiety, depression and other negative emotions have a detrimental effect on the child. Studies indicate that stress experienced by the mother during pregnancy can lead to emotional problems, conduct disorder, attention deficit and impaired cognitive development in the child. A safe, warm, supportive relationship between parents is significantly important for the development of the EI of children.

Parents have to be conscious about the fact that their own fears, insecurities and emotional needs can influence their behaviour towards the child. Many parents are ignorant of these drivers and thereby constantly justify their behaviour. Emotional needs can vary from child to child, and it is the duty of parents to recognize and fulfil them. If the emotional reservoir of the child is left dry, it can severely harm the overall development.

One of the major challenges faced by parents while dealing with teenagers is the lack of understanding of their thoughts and feelings. In the absence of emotional support at home, a growing teenager searches for support outside the family. This is one of the main reasons why many parents lose their teenage children to the outside world. It is important to see the world through the eyes of a teenager in order to understand them. This demands a high EI from parents.

Circle of Social Acceptability

One of the challenges in bringing up children, especially during the formative stages, is to manage their socially acceptable behaviour.

Socially acceptable behaviour is predominantly created by communication in the form of restrictions, guidance and teaching that we offer to our children. Challenges in this aspect of upbringing are many. Socially acceptable behaviour varies according to society, community, country and religion. There is no prescribed, defined circle. There is no benchmark to follow, and hence, parents discover their social acceptability circle driven by trial and error, and their own experiences. The circle tends to change from one generation to

Restricted/Unrestricted Behaviour

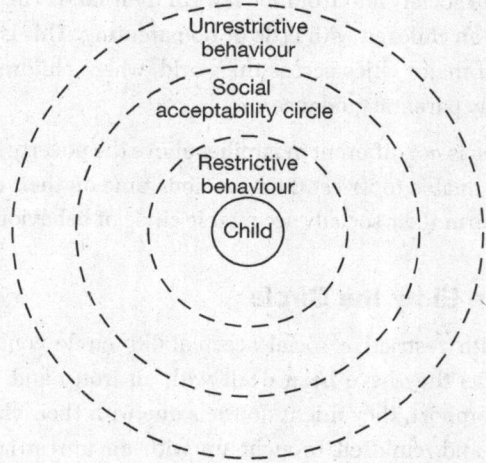

another. What was perceived as unacceptable behaviour by the earlier generation can be the norm for the next generation.

Restricted Social Acceptability Circle

If parenting involves restricting the behaviour of the child, with many 'dos and don'ts' at a formative age, it influences the overall behaviour of the child. The child, at a later stage in life, either leads a life confined to the limited circle, basically a constricted and introverted life, or rebels to break free from the shackles of social norms with a vengeance.

Unrestricted Social Acceptability Circle

If parenting is completely devoid of control or imposes minimal restrictions in the form of 'do's and don'ts' in the formative stages, the child ends up thinking that it is acceptable to break the rules and norms of society. These children would be ignorant of social norms, as they have not been programmed for the same. They inevitably face censure from society and from the laws of their land. This is a major implication on children with little or no parenting. This is evident in the slums of major cities across the world, where children grow up devoid of any parental guidance.

The situation is not different in families above the poverty line, where parents are unable to invest their precious time on their children to help them form their socially acceptable circle of behaviour.

Impact on EI by the Circle

Children with restrictive social acceptability circle could have an eroded EI, as they have been dealt with an iron hand. Devoid of emotional support, they might do the same with their children. On the other hand, children brought up with an unrestrictive social acceptability circle might lack the key components of EI as they have not been educated on the same. Finding and sticking to the golden mean in the social acceptability circle is the key to building strong EI. After all, we are in a society where interacting with people is inevitable. Being connected with each other and working together effectively is an essential part of our lives.

Learning Approach to EI

The approach to learning and building EI is dealt with in three different stages in this book, namely why, what and how. These steps help us navigate through the process effortlessly. This sequence is important for all key behavioural learnings and changes. The human mind is most conducive to this pattern of learning, as it is logical and persuasive.

Why: We have to first understand 'why' EI is important in our personal and professional lives and realize the consequences of not investing in its development. Once the 'why' is addressed, we are likely to have a higher resolve in building our EI-related competencies. A need for a strong initial buy-in for behavioural change is inevitable.

What: The understanding of 'what' is EI and its components is a very important second step. In this section, we will have to thoroughly grasp the meaning of each of the components of EI. It is imperative to understand various effective and ineffective behaviours associated with each component. This further helps in reinforcing the learning.

How: This is the most challenging part of mastering EI. From the cognitive domain of 'why' and 'what', we have to move towards the 'how' by practising behaviours that drive the development of EI. There is comparatively less literature on the development of EI, and this book would attempt to bridge that gap. Developing EI in all walks of life needs a strong resolve for self-development and disciplined practice. Over a period of time, the mind will gradually be conditioned to manage emotions better. The initial conscious efforts would gradually lead to an unconscious demonstration of better emotional management. The exercises prescribed in this book will undoubtedly help to build and nurture a strong EI.

Salient Points

- EI is important for our overall happiness and well-being.
- The components of EI—self-awareness, self-regulation, motivation, empathy and social skills—impact a host of other human competencies.
- Parenting plays an important role in developing EI in children.
- The path towards EI is understanding why EI is important, what EI is and how it could be developed.

2

Why EI?

Knowing oneself is essential for developing EI. Contributory factors in the development of EI include our life experiences, upbringing, dramatic events, education, major successes, failures, hopes and aspirations. Emotions are complex and are influenced by our feelings and reactions to various environmental stimuli. Our feelings and reactions make or mar our relationships and our overall well-being. Emotions, negative or positive, strongly impact our lives on a continuous basis.

The intensity of emotions can vary from being strong to being mild, depending on the stimulus and the way we manage them. Our level of psychological well-being can be measured by the impact of these emotions. Each individual reacts to situations differently on the basis of their EI. Reactions to emotions can vary on the basis of our 'emotional residue' at that particular point of time. Hence, we cannot afford to just drift into a sea of emotions and expect to sail through it seamlessly. It is imperative for us to learn to manage our emotions intelligently.

Let's take a look at the following example to understand this.

Through a mundane incident of everyday life, I had the opportunity to observe two distinctly different behaviours of my neighbours who once lived on either side of my apartment.

One morning, while I was on my way back after completing my cycling schedule, I noticed that my neighbour Ramesh was looking very upset, as a visitor had parked the car in his assigned parking lot. He was yelling at the top of his voice, filled with anger at the security guard and insisted that the person responsible should be summoned immediately.

After a while, the visitor who had parked his car appeared from the apartment building. Ramesh continued his verbal assault at the visitor upsetting him too. An argument erupted that lasted for more than half an hour. Subsequently, the visitor removed the vehicle, but only after an ugly scene. Ramesh walked away in a huff, consumed with anger. From what I know of him, he most likely would have carried his anger back home and spent the next several hours spitting venom at his family members. This confirmed how this particular neighbour of mine addressed most of the issues in the apartment premises. He had a 'touch me not' label and very few residents would interact with him. His family practically lived in isolation in the building.

A few weeks later, I noticed a similar incident in which a visitor parked his vehicle in the car park allocated to my other neighbour Vignesh. He enquired with the security guard about the apartment the visitor was hosted in. He rang the bell of the apartment and when the owner opened the door, he politely wished him.

After exchanging pleasantries, he mentioned that the visitor hosted in his flat had parked his car in the parking lot allocated to him. There was an instant apologetic expression on the face of the flat owner. He quickly rushed to get the car keys to remove the car. He further apologized for the inconvenience caused and assured him that the visitor shall be informed about the right parking space in the future. Vignesh had a cordial relationship with the other apartment owners and was highly respected. He would interact with all residents with ease and rarely displayed anger or frustration.

The aforementioned two narratives portray different responses to a similar situation. These two incidents summarized EI for me. Ramesh was unable to manage his emotions, leading to frustration and anger, impacting his social relationships. We can expand this example to all walks of life and realize the importance of developing EI. Nothing is worth it if you are not happy. As Dr Robert Holden, British psychologist, author and broadcaster said, 'Your relationship with yourself sets the tone for every other relationship you have.'

Our emotions create both psychological and physiological responses in us. When we are angry, it is a psychological state triggered by our emotions. The way we respond to the world around us is based on the way we manage our emotions. EI is, therefore, a very important competency for effective leadership and parenting. To excel in our professional lives or to be an achiever in any field, it is imperative to work on strengthening our EI.

Emotional Ripple

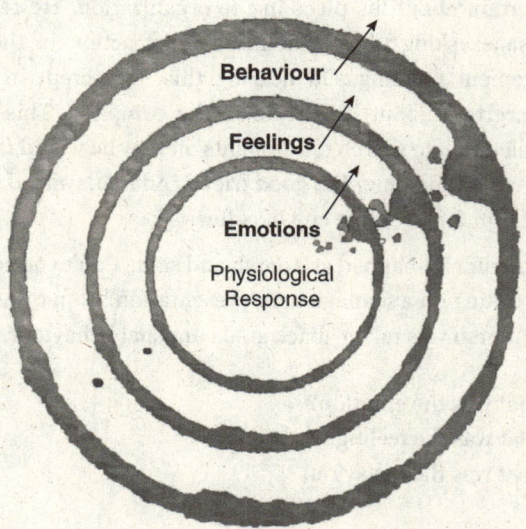

EI is about the relationship between emotions, feelings and behaviour. At times, behaviour is unpredictable and unrelated to the emotion. Hence, it is important to address the emotion rather than the behaviour. If not addressed, they do not serve us well. Unmanaged EI impacts our reactions, our attitude towards challenges and relationships.

Emotions need not be a threat all the time. It can also be a source of creation. Emotions are very much at play, be it in movie making, writing a novel, penning poetry, singing songs or any other form of creative expression. Poetry is nothing but a form of expression of our emotions and feelings. It takes a beautiful form as emotions are channelized.

Case on Emotional Ripple

Abhinav is a sales manager in a large technology company. He missed achieving his target for three consecutive quarters. He is uncertain about his place in the organization. He received a message asking to present his plan of action in the next management meeting. On hearing this, fear crept in as he was uncertain about his future in the company. This worry compelled him to search for thoughts on how he would face the management meeting. His good friend, Adarsh, walked in and invited him for a routine cup of coffee.

Abhinav rudely snapped at Adarsh and said, 'Can't you see that I am working on a management presentation? Don't waste my time.' Adarsh was taken aback at his unusual behaviour.

(E) What was the emotion?
(F) What was the feeling?
(B) What was the behaviour?

Think of an instance when you had demonstrated ineffective behaviour in the last 12 months. Try to identify the following:

The emotion experienced

_____

The feeling experienced

_____

The behaviour demonstrated

_____

Choosing a Leader

Whom do you wish to have as your leader?

Read the description listed in Options A and B. Please choose one of the options, on the basis of whom you would choose as your leader.

Option A	Option B
– Can solve mathematical problems	– Tries to understand you
– Scored high marks in school	– Listens with intent
– Solve crossword puzzle	– Influences you positively when feeling low
– Can remember facts and figures	– Takes responsibility when the chips are down
– Can analyse a problem	– Is clam in crisis situations
– Has a good range of vocabulary	– Coaches and mentors
– Can speak multiple languages	– Empathizes well
– Has a good handwriting	– Communicates clearly
– Can remember quotes and narrate them	– Knows when to say what

It has been observed that the majority choose Option B. The irony is that the education system and the selection process in most organizations focus on Option A, whereas our expectations from a leader are completely different. Our education system is not designed to produce leaders, as it focuses predominantly on the development of logical and mathematical intelligence. Option A reflects IQ and option B reflects EI-related traits. Daniel Goleman states, 'Emotional intelligence is the sine qua non of leadership. Without it, a person can have the best training in the world, an incisive, analytical mind and an endless supply of smart ideas, but he still won't make a great leader.'

EI: The Escape Velocity

The right analogy is 'escape velocity'. It is defined as the velocity any object needs to travel and to get out of the grip of earth's gravity. Similarly, the elements of EI, namely self-awareness, self-regulation, motivation, empathy and social skills, allow us to escape from the ordinary. They allow us to catapult the benefits of our functional and technical competencies to a higher plane.

The other analogy is that of a rocket, trying to escape from the gravitational pull of the earth. The fuel of the rocket is EI, and the body of the rocket represents functional and technical skills. The thrust of the engine can be equated to EI, which helps the rocket escape from the gravity of ineffectiveness. In other words, EI fuel propels us to greater heights, far higher than the ordinary fuel.

Majority of the energy is spent by a rocket in achieving escape velocity and once it is free from the gravitational force of the earth, the vehicle operates with high efficiency. Similarly, once we break free from ineffective behaviour, we can gain higher achievements. IQ can take us on the path of success to a certain extent, but the escape velocity will take us to a completely different orbit. Daniel Goleman, the father of EI, attributes 20 per cent probability to IQ and 80 per cent to EI.

During the initial stages of life, while receiving formal education, IQ matters to a great extent. As we proceed further into the journey of

IQ versus EQ

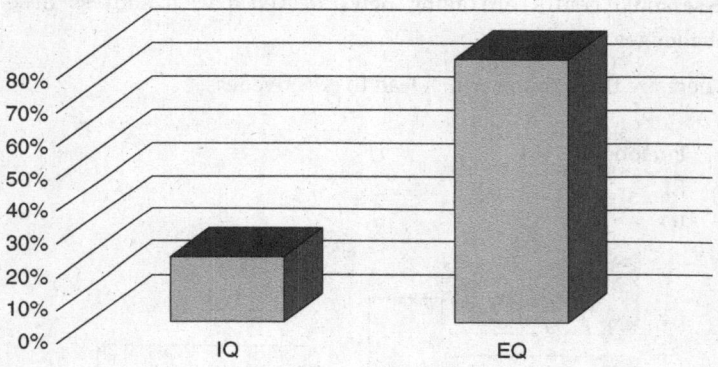

our lives, the relevance of EI gains higher importance over IQ. This is the reason why some of the academically average students tend to perform better in both personal and professional lives. The real challenges in life commence when we start interacting and working with people and managing challenging situations.

The importance of EI gradually increases in our professional and personal lives. Techno-functional expertise plays a higher role during the initial stages of our career, and EI gradually takes over as the major contributor to our success.

Despite this, few organizations invest in the assessment or development of EI. As well said by Dr Stephen Covey, 'We tend to hire people for their functional skills and fire for behaviour.' The predominant reason for this is the difficulty in assessing people on EI.

Some of the assessment tools available are psychometric tests, behavioural event interviews and reference checks apart from conducting an 'assessment centre'. Brick and mortar assessment centres are difficult to administer for new hires, as we need a sizeable number of candidates for conducting them. Online digital assessment centres are taking their deserved space to address these challenges.

There are three things which lead to effectiveness:

- Personality
- EI
- IQ

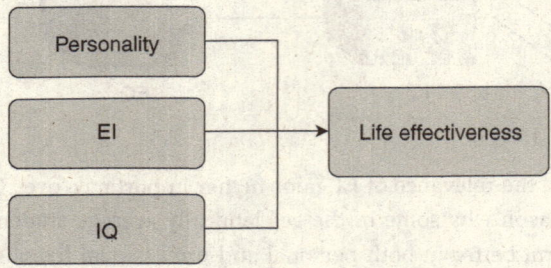

All the aforementioned traits determine our effectiveness in our professional and personal lives.

We use the aforementioned three aspects in varying degrees in our everyday lives. Personality and IQ do not predict the strength of our EI as it is a unique intelligence and hence needs specific attention. All three factors operate independently and have less correlation. Irrespective of an individual's personality and IQ, EI can be high or low.

Types of Emotions

We experience a variety of emotions in our daily lives. These emotions can be categorized into positive and negative. There are seven basic emotions, namely anger, happiness, fear, disgust, surprise, love and sadness.

Negative emotions are etched in our memory and are much stronger than positive ones. EI is a part of positive psychology that helps mould human behaviour and makes us capable of effectively managing the challenges we face in our lives. Due to our survival instinct, negative emotions are etched in our memory stronger than positive emotions.

Emotional Residue

This exercise is designed to understand the emotional residue that we carry on the basis of our experiences from the incidents that we encounter in our lives. When we minimize negative emotions and create a positive emotional residue, it is likely to lead us towards happiness, good health and good relationships.

Negative emotional residue, undisputedly, leads to unhappiness, ill-health and sore relationships. Choosing our emotions at every single moment in our lives is entirely in our control. In other words, it is the choices we make at every stage that create positive or negative emotional residue.

Emotional Residue

Positive Emotions	Negative Emotions	Emotional Residue
• Appreciation	• Resentment	(+) Emotional residue
• Satisfaction	• Anger	
• Love	• Failure	• Happiness
• Recognition	• Disappoinment	• Good health
• Happiness	• Guilt	• Good relationship
• Bonding	• Frustration	• Prosperity and growth
• Realization	• Obligation	
• Awareness	• Bitterness	(−) Emotional residue
• Contentment	• Loneliness	
• Joy	• Depression	• Sorrow
• Peace	• Lethargy	• Ill health
		• Strained relationship
		• Poverty and stagnation

In the absence of the management of emotions, we further reinforce our thoughts 'I am ok, you and all others are not ok.' We tend to get caught in this vicious cycle if we leave our emotions unmanaged.

Developing EI involves 'emotional sensitivity'. The antenna of the mind should be sensitive enough to receive emotional signals in self and others. If the signals are cut off and there is less or no reception, the management of emotions, such as processing, thinking, being aware and responding in the right manner, is not likely to happen.

My Emotional Residue

Note down the emotions experienced in the recent past (1–12 months) on the basis of the incidents you encountered.

Key Emotions

Contentment, anger, appreciation, awareness, bitterness, bonding, depression, disappointment, failure, frustration, guilt, happiness, joy, lethargy, loneliness, love, obligation, peace, realization, recognition, resentment and satisfaction.

Note down the emotions experienced in the recent past (1–12 months). Place a tick mark against the emotion experienced.		
S. No.	**Emotional Entries**	✓
1	I got angry with someone.	
2	I felt like celebrating.	
3	I felt sad.	
4	I felt being loved.	
5	I felt lonely.	
6	I felt I will be successful.	

S. No.	Emotional Entries	✓
7	I felt that I am not good enough.	
8	I felt that I have done well.	
9	I felt that I can't succeed.	
10	I was happy with the outcome.	
11	I felt others are better than me.	
12	I felt being wanted.	
13	I felt disappointed.	
14	I felt a sense of achievement.	
15	I felt ignored.	
16	I felt like smiling.	
17	I felt hopeless.	
18	I enjoyed the company of people around.	
19	I felt not being loved.	
20	I was appreciated by others.	
21	I felt I had made mistakes.	
22	I received recognition.	
23	I hated the way someone behaved.	
24	Felt that I can make it big.	
25	I felt that nothing is going good for me.	
26	I was respected.	
27	I felt nothing is possible.	
28	I was heard.	

Write down the type of emotions experienced, on the basis of the responses chosen. Mark whether the emotion was positive or negative. Provide (+1) for each positive emotion and (−1) for each negative emotion. Add up the total of positive and negative, and arrive at the final score.

If your score is negative, you are carrying a 'negative emotional residue'. This indicates that you have emotional scars left behind on the basis of the incidents experienced by you in your recent past.

If your score is positive, it indicates that you have a 'positive emotional residue' and that you have managed your emotions well. There are lesser emotional scars left behind by your recent experiences.

This exercise can be repeated, going further back into your past. You will be able to realize the emotional residual baggage you are carrying around.

After extensive research, Dr James Pennebaker, an American social psychologist, found that writing down our emotional experiences enhances our physical and mental well-being. When we do this, we tend to develop insights into our emotions and feelings, making it easier to manage them.

We often have a tendency to typecast emotions by labelling people, for example, a particularly unpleasant person of being angry perennially. If we dig deeper, there are many other emotions that a person experiences. If we strive to understand this aspect in us and in others, we have a good opportunity to manage emotions effectively and build better relationships.

Dr Susan David listed some of the commonly experienced emotions in humans and categorized them into anger, sadness, anxiety, hurt, embarrassment and happiness.

Benefits of EI

Developing and driving our lives with EI bestows numerous benefits in our lives. EI is an intrinsic part of positive psychology that adds

List of Common Emotions

Anger	Sadness	Anxiety	Hurt	Embarrassment	Happiness
Grumpy	Disappointed	Afraid	Jealous	Isolated	Thankful
Frustrated	Mournful	Stressed	Betrayed	Self-conscious	Trusting
Annoyed	Regretful	Vulnerable	Isolated	Lonely	Comfortable
Defensive	Depressed	Confused	Shocked	Inferior	Content
Vindictive	helpless	Panicky	Deprived	Guilty	Excited
Impatient	Pessimistic	Sceptical	Victimized	Ashamed	Relaxed
Disgusted	Tearful	Worried	Aggrieved	Unacceptable	Relieved
Offended	Terrified	Cautious	Tormented	Pitiable	Overjoyed
Irritated	Disillusioned	Nervous	Abandoned	Confused	Confident

Source: David (2019).

greater value to our personality and to our IQ. The tasteful cocktail of all three offers immense benefits, which are as follows:

- Reduced stress levels
- Effective conflict management
- Enhanced relationship—interpersonal skills
- Enthusiastic work environment
- Enhanced leadership skills
- Improved responses
- Higher creativity
- Improved clarity of thinking
- Increased productivity
- Effective problem-solving
- Effective decision-making

The higher the level of leadership in the organization, the greater the importance of EI. At lower levels of leadership, more functional skills come into play.

EI Pyramid

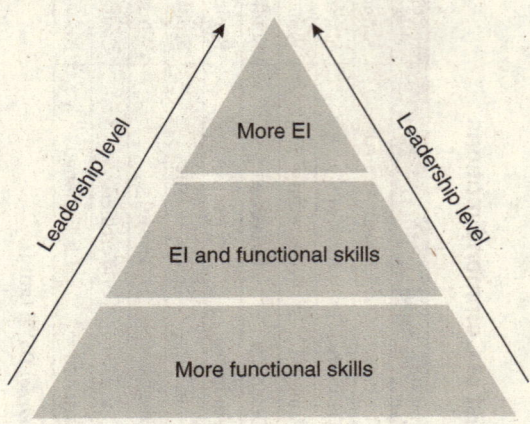

Benefits of EI

Think of a recent situation which made you unhappy.

_____

_____

What was the trigger of the unhappiness?

_____

_____

What was the impact of your unhappiness on you and people around you?

_____

_____

If you look back, could you have handled the situation differently?

_____

_____

If the situation was handled differently, what would have been your emotion?

_____

_____

This exercise gives us a perspective that if we had exercised a more effective choice, a positive outcome could have been achieved.

If we want positive emotions to occupy our lives, it is important for us to work on the source. It is obvious that EI is one of the most powerful competencies to develop.

Salient Points

- EI is the relationship among emotions, feelings and behaviour.
- Becoming emotionally intelligent through self-awareness, self-regulation, motivation, social skills and empathy offers the required velocity to help us escape from the ordinary.
- Maintaining an emotional diary helps us create positive emotional residue.
- EI offers diverse benefits such as enhanced relationships, leadership skills, effective conflict management, decision-making and problem-solving, reduced stress levels and higher creativity.

3 What Is EI?

E I is the reception of a stimulus from the environment with an awareness of emotions in oneself and others which helps us make considered choices. It is about striking a balance between emotions and rationale, thereby positively influencing human interactions and decision-making.

Decoding EI

1. Reception of stimulus

2. Emotional awareness in self and others

3. Choices based on emotional and rational balance

4. Effective human interaction and decision-making

- **Happiness**
- **Good health**
- **Good relationship**
- **Prosperity and growth**

EI constitutes of five main components and several elements rested within each component. This signifies the width of the impact that EI has on diverse sets of human behaviour.

Understanding EI

EI is a social–emotional competence. EI as a model can be broken into two broad aspects:

1. Managing self
2. Managing others

The process of demonstrating EI commences with 'managing self', followed by 'managing others'. 'Managing others' is unlikely to be effective until 'managing self' is achieved. The inherent effectiveness is driven by the 'core' of managing self. The best analogy from nature would be the 'core of the earth'. The earth's magnetic field is created in the swirling outer core, as the planet rotates steadily at a speed of 1,040 miles per hour. This magnetic field is crucial to life on our planet. It protects the earth from the charged particles of the solar wind. Without the shield of the magnetic field, the solar wind would strip the earth's atmosphere of the ozone layer that protects life from harmful ultraviolet radiation.

Similarly, in EI, effectiveness starts with the core, which is 'managing self'. Effective self-management creates the required magnetism to manage others effectively. In other words, one must first work on 'oneself' in order to positively influence 'others'. Another way to understand this is with the help of the railway train analogy. The

Engine of EI

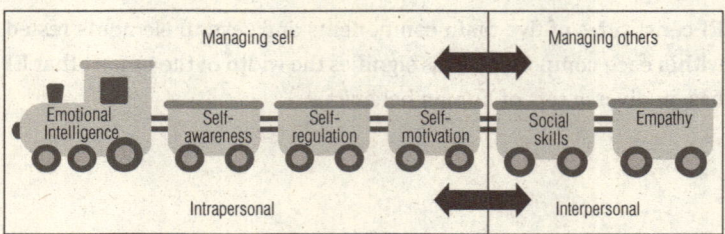

sequence of managing emotions starts with self-awareness, followed by self-regulation and then self-motivation. The engine of EI is powered by managing 'self' first, which in turn brings together the components of social skills and empathy. Unless we develop our intrapersonal skills (managing self), it is unlikely that we can ever demonstrate interpersonal skills (managing others).

Managing Self

Managing self is about being aware of the emotions experienced by us and managing them well. If managing self is not achieved effectively, the journey of developing EI is stunted.

Managing self has three main components that constitute EI in humans:

1. Self-awareness
2. Self-regulation
3. Self-motivation

The keyword here is 'self'. Unless self-awareness is built, it is not possible to achieve self-regulation. When self-awareness, self-regulation and self-motivation are effectively put in place, our internal locus of control towards achievement orientation is triggered.

The Impact of Moods

It is a well-established fact that moods influence the emotions of people around us. If the brain's limbic system, which is our emotional centre, is a closed-loop system, it drives a regulated emotional response. If it is an open loop, then we need external help in managing our emotions. Moods are determined by our connections with other people. Research indicates that emotions can be triggered even among strangers. People can influence one another, despite not speaking a word to each other, just through body language and communication.

EI and Leadership

Our experiences tell us that many intelligent people tend to fail when they are placed in critical leadership positions. This questions the conventional understanding of human intelligence. Leaders with different individual styles have been successful in various walks of life. But one thing common in them is high EI.

EI and Decision-making

Decision-making is one of the important responsibilities of a leader. Senior leaders make many decisions that have far-reaching consequences across the organization. Our brain tends to recognize a set of patterns, on the basis of which we make a decision. A chess player predicts the pattern on the basis of the current positions and moves of the opponent.

If negative emotional impulses interfere during pattern recognition, it is likely to disrupt our analytical ability. If emotions overtake our thinking process and freeze rational thinking, then the decision is likely to be ineffective. Decisions taken only on the basis of rationality, devoid of any emotions, are also likely to fail.

If the decision-making process is not driven by an emotional feel for the subject, there could be a prolonged analysis with no effective decision taken. Striking a balance between rational thinking and emotional feel for the subject is needed for effective decision-making.

Can EI be Learnt?

EI is both acquired and learnt. It can be built through a deep understanding of the lessons learnt from life experiences. On the

EI Construct

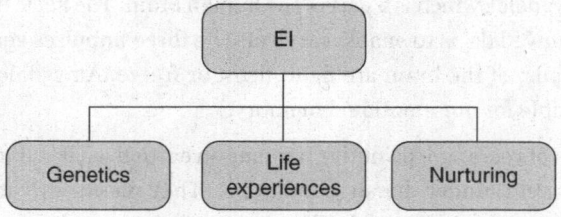

other hand, genetics too play an important role in the development of EI.

It is rather difficult to peg a percentage on the contribution of genetics and life experiences in the development of EI. With age and maturity, EI tends to get stronger.

Amygdala Hijack

Amygdala, a part of the limbic system, is an almond-shaped set of neurons, located deep in the brain's medial temporal lobe. It plays a key role in the processing of emotions.

Amygdala is located in the midbrain. A significant research by Joseph LeDoux, an American neuroscientist, established the role of the amygdala in emotional reactions and memories. Patients with lesions or other injuries to the right amygdala showed loss of emotional self-awareness.

For someone with a strong EI, any road rage incident would seem extremely ridiculous and senseless. When provoked on the road, even educated people who are not emotionally intelligent are engulfed at times and get into a street fight. For those involved in road rage incidents, their effort to prove their point is a life-and-death situation at that moment. Their response is an emotional discharge, with no reasoning or logic. Where does this instant reaction come from?

To understand this emotion, it is important to know the function of the 'amygdala', which is a part of the human brain. The basic function of the 'amygdala' is to enable survival. The three impulses generated by this part of the brain are fight, flight or freeze. Amygdala is also responsible for our emotional memory.

Millions of years ago, primitive humans on earth lived in a dangerous environment under harsh conditions. They faced threats from predators, the climate and other human beings, and they had to strive to survive. Under these threatening situations, amygdala shuts the rational part of the brain from thinking. It creates an emotional memory of the threats faced in the past.

When the primitive man walked into the jungle and heard a rustling noise in the bushes and suddenly found himself facing a tiger, he was compelled to run and climb a tree. This emotional memory, triggering a spontaneous response, is already registered by the amygdala. The next time he heard a rustling noise from the bushes, the memory would be quickly recalled for choosing the fight, flight or freeze response. Humans could survive life-threatening situations in the primitive stages of evolution with the help of this instant response system controlled by the amygdala. This mechanism of fear and anxiety has helped man to survive. In the absence of this mechanism, the humankind would have engaged in perilous acts and put its survival at peril. Hence, fear and anxiety are important emotions that helped us survive the dangers. If fear takes over our judgement and decision-making, then it would be counterproductive. Fear as an emotion helps us to plan and prepare for the uncertainties of the future. The challenge is when it overcomes us and the emotion is sustained for a long period of time. It leads to perennial stress and anxiety that would make us unhappy.

When there is an amygdala hijack, the heartbeat increases, blood pressure rises and the person is ready for the fight, flight or freeze response. This is caused by the adrenaline rush into the bloodstream.

Increased adrenaline causes an increase in the supply of oxygen and glucose to the muscles, enabling them to act quickly. All these actions are controlled by the limbic and reptilian brain.

During the amygdala hijack, the brain shuts the digestive system, thereby saving significant amounts of energy. It also shuts down the communication system and hence we struggle to find the right words. In a lighter vein, this primitive mechanism understood that silence is a better virtue to have when in danger.

Neocortex in the modern brain does not realize this. The ability to hear oneself reduces, probably to pay more attention to other noises thought to be posing a danger. During a crisis or under stress, the brain can register high-frequency noises and less of one's voice.

When stress levels are high, the ability to read the body language of other humans reduces. Acute stress minimizes our capacity to read other people's emotions and feelings. Self-regulation is nothing but learning to effectively balance and get back to normal through enhanced awareness. It is during such moments that learning happens the most.

Anger can manifest itself in the form of frustration, stress, anxiety, confusion, embarrassment, jealousy, rejection and threat. When anger gains momentum, it pushes us further, leading us to a state of aggression. If this is not managed effectively, it is likely to lead to consequences that could defame us, impact our image, self-esteem and cause physical harm.

Cortisol, a hormone which is released in response to stress, can only be flushed out of the body through sweat, urine and tears. That's the reason we usually feel relieved when we cry, as the accumulated cortisol is released in the form of tears.

In the modern world, the amygdala plays the same role of emotional memory and sensing of threat situations. The nature of threat, however, has changed significantly. We no longer live in the jungle, infested with predators in a hostile environment. We live in protected homes under the governance of law and order. This civilization is witnessing a changed set of threats. Threats in the modern world for which the amygdala is activated include social threats, financial threats and insecurities.

Some of the threats which we face in the modern world are as follows:

- What will my family do if I die?
- What will be my image in the society if I fail?
- Will I lose my promotion?
- Am I being respected?
- What if I fail in achieving my goals?
- Am I being disrespected by others?
- What will happen to the future of my children?
- Am I fit and healthy?
- How would I face unpredictable financial burden?
- What if I am not ignored?
- Will I be lonely in old age?
- Am I looking good?
- Am I accepted by others?

The list is endless. The threat to life in the past has now changed to a mental threat. In many instances, it is imaginary and is about the future or the past. Imagine experiencing similar reactions in our body when we are faced with the threats of the modern world. The amygdala is innocently unaware of the changed nature of the threat from primitive to modern times. It simply does its job. The modern world has given rise to perennial fears such as pandemics like COVID-19, war and conflicts, global economic depression cycles and destruction of the environment.

Fear is the root cause of many of our responses. Our survival mechanism triggers these fears. The situations provided further illustrate the effect of fear under different circumstances.

Emotional Root Cause and Effect

I Am Upset With	The Situation	It Affects My
My friend	He did not take notice of and involve me in the conversation. Why did he do that to me?	Self-esteem, security, pride, fear
Customer service executive	Was rude and not bothered to listen and respond to the query. I don't treat people in this manner.	Self-esteem, security, pride, fear
My boss	Was unreasonable, promoted someone else for the position I deserved. Does he hate me?	Self-esteem, financial security, pride, fear
Spouse	Defensive, justifies, does not accept faults, points mistake in me, tries to prove others wrong, wants me to be responsible for his/her happiness.	Pride, security, self-esteem, fear
Family	Do not recognise me, they are not supportive, do not understand my point of view, not concerned about my welfare.	Self-esteem, pride, fear

Following are the physiological changes in the body when the amygdala is triggered: Amygdala, when activated, based on the threat, instantly reduces the flow of blood to most parts of the brain. Heartbeat increases to facilitate more flow of blood to the brain in order to help us think and act faster. Muscles become tense to cope with the fight, flight or freeze action. The body sweats to keep itself cool for the emergency reaction.

The aforementioned physiological reactions are aimed at a quick response when danger is sensed. Dr Walter B. Cannon, an American physiologist, termed this an 'emergency reaction' in order to manage the stress of the 20th century.

The complexity in the new millennium has further enhanced and is likely to grow. This leads to severe challenges such as stress and anxiety disorders. Amygdala, which was designed to help us survive, has become the reason for ailments such as heart disease, depression and other medical disorders. From the role of a saviour, it is well on its way to becoming the destroyer, if not managed well. Self-regulation of emotions helps us make use of the amygdala for our betterment.

Stress Due to the Amygdala

The primitive human felt threatened when in danger. The frequency of threats experienced by them could not be predicted. Threats could have been experienced on a couple of occasions a day or once in two days or once a week. The emotional memory of the amygdala helped the ancient man to recognize and avoid these threats.

In the modern world, humans live constantly with anxiety, fear of the past and of the future. Threat therefore is perceived several times a day, based on how emotions are handled.

Stress Experienced by Primitive Human

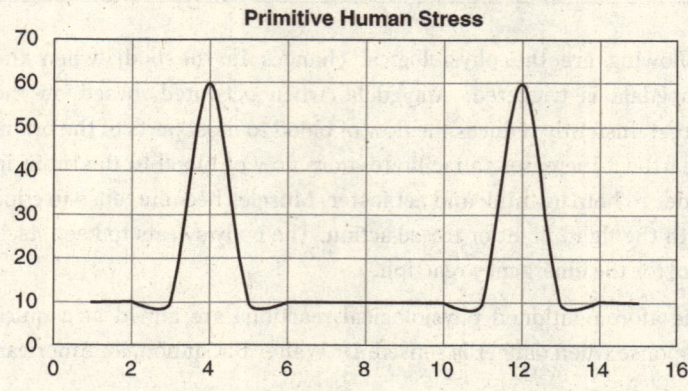

Primitive Human Stress

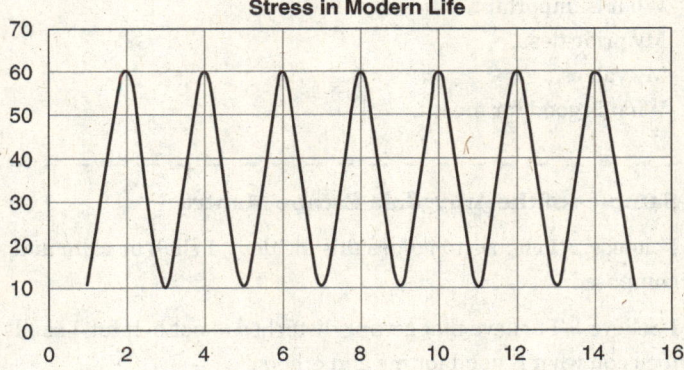
Stress in Modern Life

As per research findings, stress is one of the significant causes of ill health. Happiness is the best cure, as it enhances the immune system of the body. Chronic stress, such as anxiety and depression, raises the level of cortisol in the body, which is harmful. Elevated cortisol impacts learning and memory, lowers bone density, raises blood pressure, cholesterol and increases the risk of heart disease.

Amygdala Rescue Mantra

In order to escape from 'amygdala hijack', we need to take a pause. During the hijack, we tend to act devoid of any rational thinking and often repent on our words and actions. One of the effective ways to escape from the clutches of the hijack is to practise what is called the 'amygdala rescue mantra'.

Mantras, originally practised in Hinduism and Buddhism, are repetitive recitals to help us to concentrate or meditate. We can choose to create our own mantra. The repeated recital of the mantra has a calming influence on the brain. These are some of the keywords for creating our own mantra.

- I choose...
- I believe...

- What is important...
- My priorities...
- My values...
- What is good for me is...

Samples of the Amygdala Escape Mantra

I choose... 'I choose to ignore this incident, I shall be calm and composed.'

I believe... 'I believe that getting disturbed is not helpful, I shall focus on what is good for me and others.'

What is important... 'My family members and their happiness is important to me, I shall keep them happy.'

My priorities... 'My priority is not to win this argument. It is to get the job done.'

My values... 'I shall always respect people, I shall be truthful.'

What is good for me is... 'My happiness and good health. I shall not let incidences/experiences impact it.'

Draft down your amygdala escape mantra.

_____

_____

_____

_____

Recite this mantra whenever your emotions overpower you, or when your emotions are getting out of your control. This would help in calming the mind. If the mantra is recited after a few deep breaths, it would have a greater impact in managing emotions.

Balance between Emotions and Rationality

Emotions are drivers of our behaviour. Managing emotions is different from 'being emotional'. Being emotional is often used in a negative sense. It implies that we are driven by our emotions, thereby drifting in the cloud of indecisiveness.

When a decision is purely based on emotions, devoid of any rationale, it most probably turns out to be ineffective. The same applies to the contrary. Effective decision-making is about striking a balance between 'emotional and rational thinking'.

Insight into EI Model

The EI model is essentially built on understanding, building and driving EI. The components of EI, namely self-awareness, self-regulation,

EI Model

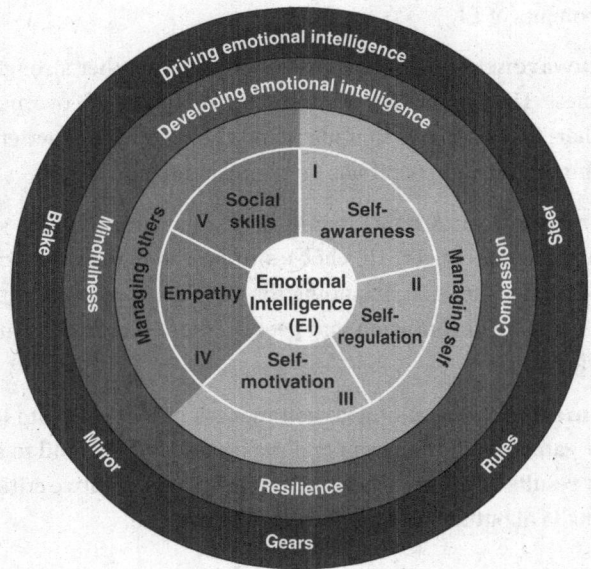

self-motivation, empathy and social skills, have an interdependent sequence. Each component leads to another. The development process needs to necessarily follow this sequence for the better demonstration of EI.

The development of EI requires focus on mindfulness, resilience and compassion. These components help us build the fuel necessary for driving EI. Steps for driving EI can be explained with the analogy of driving a car using brake, mirrors, gears, rules and steer. This is explained in detail later in the book.

EI COMPONENTS—BEHAVIOUR IN ACTION

EI can be broken down into the following five components. It also indicates 'what it means' and the evidence of the components.

The following behaviour in action can be observed for each of the components of EI.

Self-awareness: The manager understands his/her strengths and weakness. He/she realizes when his/her emotions are overpowering him/her, takes a pause to understand the emotions experienced by him/her and the impact it has on the team members.

Self-regulation: A father, while discussing career choices with his son, experiences anger. He chooses to postpone the discussion. He considers the situation, including the people around at that point of time, the state of confusion and peer pressure that his son might be experiencing.

Self-motivation: An athlete commences practice despite losing a major game by a thin margin and makes up his/her mind to achieve better results in the next match. He/she ignores negative criticism in the media about the way he/she played the game.

Components of EI

EI Component	What It Signifies	Evidence
Self-awareness	Ability to read our own emotions well captures the stimulus from others effectively	• Knowing ones strengths and limitations • Self-confidence • Recognizing mistakes
Self-regulation	Ability to manage our emotions when faced with negative and positive stimulus from the environment	• Calm and composed • Making considered decisions • Open to change • Not ruled by external stimulus
Self-motivation	Drive and perseverance towards goals despite all odds	• Not giving up easily • Pursue goals • Manage impediments
Empathy	Being receptive to the emotions experienced by others	• Listening with intent • Coach and mentor • Understanding others • Bringing comfort to people
Social skills	Building trust and demonstrating interpersonal skills with others	• Building social network • Ability to get things done through people • Leading teams effectively

Empathy: A mother intuitively recognizes what her daughter is going through, even though she does not discuss her feelings with her. She tries to understand what is bothering her and provides solace and comfort.

Social skill: A lady recruit to the company proactively connects with people and offers to help. She lends support to people requiring help spontaneously. She is able to influence teams in major decisions. She is in constant touch with the stakeholder to get things done for her team.

Salient Points

- EI constitutes two main factors: 'managing self' and 'managing others'.
- Managing 'self' precedes managing 'others'.
- 'Amygdala hijack' due to fear and anxiety creates stressful situations. We must learn to manage it better, as over time it works in the modern world.
- 'Amygdala rescue mantra' can help us escape the 'amygdala hijack'.
- EI is balancing 'emotional' and 'rational' thinking.

4 Self-awareness

Understanding Self-awareness

Self-awareness is the first step towards EI. Self-awareness involves having a deep understanding of one's emotions, thoughts, behaviour, strengths, weaknesses, needs and drives. It's about being aware of our psychological state of mind at any given point of time.

Self-awareness should not be grossly unrealistic nor hopelessly pessimistic. We need to strike a golden mean by being honest and realistic with the help of accurate self-assessment.

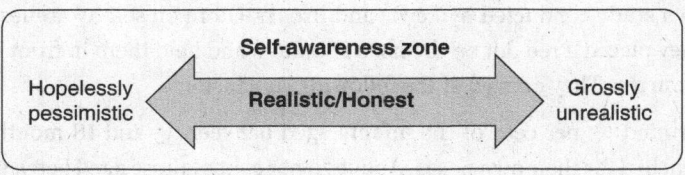

People with a high level of self-awareness recognize not only their own feelings but also that of people around them. They are more equipped to face demanding situations, as they would be able to consciously choose the right responses. Understanding of one's values plays a major role here. People with self-awareness are more likely to make choices driven by their values and goals, rather than by circumstances and environmental triggers.

A high level of self-awareness leads to more accurate self-assessment. It makes us capable of demonstrating a self-deprecating sense of humour and to be more comfortable discussing our own limitations. It enables us to be open to constructive feedback. On the contrary, those with low self-awareness would view such feedback as a threat or as a sign of failure.

People with a high level of self-awareness can be well recognized by their self-confidence. They are unlikely to give up when faced with challenging situations. They do not hesitate reaching out for help from others to get things done.

With a high level of self-awareness, we will naturally give credit to where it belongs and acknowledge those who contribute. We would also have the capacity to self-assess in a realistic manner, leading to development.

Our lives would be in turmoil if we fail to understand our own emotions and feelings. Self-awareness can be developed by being open to receiving feedback. All other components of EI germinate from self-awareness and its absence would insulate us from further developing our EI.

In a study conducted by Lewis and Brooks-Gunn on self-awareness, they placed a red dot on the nose of infants and held them in front of a mirror. They arrived at the following conclusions.

Around 25 per cent of the infants aged between 15 and 18 months reached for their own noses. About 70 per cent of those aged between 21 and 24 months also did the same. This shows that children develop some kind of self-awareness after the age of 15 to 18 months. Infants of age less than 12 months are unlikely to be self-aware. This experiment pertains to visual self-awareness. There are many other dimensions of self-awareness.

Being self-aware is unique to human beings. Animals are devoid of this intelligence. There are traces of self-awareness evident in chimpanzees. It is suggested by researchers that the anterior cingulate cortex, located in the frontal lobe of the human brain, plays an important role in self-awareness.

Humans have the unique capability of getting out of their bodies and visualizing themselves. This ability is important for the development of our EI. With the help of self-awareness, we become aware of our strengths, weaknesses and limitations. The most significant part of this capability is the ability to remain aware of the emotions that we experience and identify the causes for the same.

Self-awareness is a strong predictor of our effectiveness in life. We can identify opportunities, threats and other related signals in a more effective manner and choose what is appropriate for us. We are often caught in the rigmarole of our daily lives and tend to avoid self-reflection until we are faced with severe challenges and failures.

Emotions and Feelings

Emotions are instinctive responses coming out of the amygdala, the limbic system of the brain. These responses generate biochemical and electrical reactions, basically neurological reactions to a stimulus.

Imagine a mother waiting for her child to come back from school and is worried about the unusual delay. The moment she sees the child, the feelings experienced by her will help us to understand instinctive emotions.

Emotions can be conscious or unconscious. We could lead our entire lives without understanding some of the emotions experienced by us. The mother might just run to hug the child in relief, without being conscious of her surroundings.

Feelings are bodily reactions that are triggered by the activities of neurotransmitters and hormones. These are released into the brain, lending a conscious experience. In other words, emotions activate feelings that can then be experienced by us.

Feelings are influenced by beliefs, memories, thoughts and past experiences. Feelings include physical sensations of touch, hunger, pain, etc. When the mother sees the child safely back from school after the delay, she experiences joy while hugging the child and finds comfort in the bodily touch.

There are three dimensions of self-awareness that can be summarized into four questions:

1. *What's happening to me?* The ability to understand what's happening in our day-to-day lives. Where am I heading towards in terms of emotions? It also involves taking account of incidents happening around us, impacting our emotions.
2. *What are my feelings?* Emotions being experienced by us on a regular basis and the feelings that are generated. It helps us to understand the link between emotions and feelings.
3. *Why am I experiencing these emotions?* Introspecting who or what is the trigger or the root cause for the emotions that are being experienced.
4. *What are the blind spots?* The ability to reflect on our blind spots, which are aspects of us that we are unaware of. It is minimizing ignorance about ourselves and knowing about the unknown self.

Being unaware of our own feelings and emotions is the highest form of emotional illiteracy. Many significant challenges are faced in the absence of self-awareness. Learning how to remain self-aware is the first significant step towards developing EI.

Types of Self-awareness

Extensive research on self-awareness has led to the identification of two distinct types. The initial school of thought termed it as *self-consciousness*. Subsequently, two different aspects were identified: internal self-awareness and external self-awareness, according to Dr Tasha Eurich.

Internal Self-awareness

This refers to how distinctly one's own thoughts, feelings, behaviour, strengths and weaknesses can be observed. It further extends to our ability to observe our own values, aspirations, passion, compatibility towards the environment and the impact on others. Higher internal self-awareness is more likely to result in better EI. Lack of it can lead to stress, lack of self-esteem and, in extreme cases, foolhardy actions.

External Self-awareness

The second dimension of self-awareness is the ability to see how others view us in the context of the same aspects mentioned earlier. It indicates that those with higher external self-awareness are more likely to display empathy towards others. They can see how other people perceive them and hence are more likely to modify their behaviour. This enhances their chances of building better relationships. They are also perceived to be effective by other people.

It is easy to assume that if we have one type of self-awareness, we are likely to be high in the other. This is not true, as they are distinctly different. One can be highly internally self-aware, but lack external self-awareness and vice versa. On the basis of the levels of these two types of self-awareness, we can further understand the types of possible behaviours.

	Low External Self-awareness	High External Self-awareness
High Internal Self-awareness	**Insulated** • Fair understanding of self • Pleased with current self • Limited self development • Limited window for feedback	**Self-aware** • Good understanding of self • Good understanding of how others perceive them • Open for feedback • High on introspection

	Low External Self-awareness	High External Self-awareness
Low Internal Self-awareness	**Self-ignorant** • Low understanding of self • Lack of understanding one's strengths and weaknesses • Dependence on assurance externally • Low understanding of others perception of self	**Amiable** • Focused on perception of others • Low in introspection • Ready to compromise self-interest • Focused on making others happy

Source: Eurich (2018).

Insulated

They are pretty clear on who they are in their own eyes. They however do not challenge their views or search for blind spots by taking feedback from others. This can harm their relationships and limit their success.

Self-aware

They know who they are, what they want to accomplish, seek out and value others' opinions. These are the leaders who fully realize the true benefits of self-awareness.

Self-ignorant

They don't yet know who they are, what they stand for or how their teams perceive them. As a result, they might feel stuck or frustrated with their performance and relationships.

Amiable

They can be so focused on appearing a certain way in the eyes of others that they could be overlooking what really matters to themselves. Over a period of time, they tend to make choices that are detrimental to their own comfort and fulfilment.

Elements of Self-awareness

There are three elements of self-awareness, namely emotional awareness, accurate self-assessment and self-confidence.

Emotional Awareness

It is about recognizing one's emotions and their effect on us. Humans are a bundle of emotions, and we experience a diverse set of emotions in our day-to-day lives. The ability to be aware of the emotions being experienced at all times is emotional awareness. Once this awareness is gained, we could make effective choices.

Accurate Self-assessment

Self-assessment is understanding one's strengths, weaknesses and limitations, leading to self-confidence. Higher the self-assessment, better would be our ability to take decisions on the basis of the choices offered.

Self-confidence

Self-confidence is having a sense of self-worth and thereby not being threatened by people and situations around them. High self-confidence increases our trust in people and enhances our ability to receive criticism and feedback gracefully.

Self-awareness cannot be developed only through experiences gained in life. At times, we remain blind to some of our habitual behavioural patterns and fail to question them. In a research conducted among managers, it was learnt that more the experience, less the ability to self-assess their leadership effectiveness.

According to Dr Tasha Eurich, when 3,600 leaders across various roles and industries were studied, it was conclusive that the more power they held, the more their tendency was to overestimate their skills and abilities in comparison with the perception of others. This pattern was reflected on 19 out of 20 competencies researched, including emotional self-awareness, accurate self-assessment, empathy, trustworthiness and leadership performance. This could most likely be due to the fact that the more senior a leader, the lesser the number of people to provide them with feedback.

More power leaders wield in organizations, lesser would be the comfort in others around them to provide them feedback. Professor James O'Toole adds that when one's power grows, one's willingness to listen shrinks, either because they think they know more than the team members or because seeking feedback comes at a cost.

This can be changed for the better. The research further indicated that most successful leaders change this tendency by seeking frequent feedback from bosses, peers and subordinates. This helps them to be internally and externally self-aware. They seek critical feedback from their superiors and subordinates, particularly from the people they trust, which helps them develop their external self-awareness in particular.

Gaining Self-awareness through Feedback

Feedback is one of the most effective ways to develop self-awareness. In an organization context, '360-degree feedback' is a very effective mechanism. Feedback can be a challenging process, as it might shake our self-perception and established thoughts about ourselves. We need a lot of courage to be open to feedback.

It is also equally important to choose the right people to seek feedback from. Those who are biased and have a hidden agenda would not be able to provide us with candid and honest feedback. They would tend to either sugar-coat or deliberately drive their

Internal versus External Self-awareness Exercise

Please attempt all the 20 statements

Please choose on the basis of what applies to you most often in your personal and professional life

1 = Never, 2 = Rarely, 3 = Sometimes, 4 = Mostly, 5 = Always

S. No.	Statements	1	2	3	4	5
1	I understand the thoughts going on in my mind.					
2	I understand how others perceive my strengths.					
3	I understand the feelings that I am experiencing.					
4	I can understand how others see me behave.					
5	I understand my own behaviour.					
6	I understand when others see mistakes in me.					
7	I understand my strengths.					
8	I can sense when others dislike me.					
9	I understand my weaknesses.					
10	I understand when others know that I am struggling.					
11	I understand my emotions.					
12	I understand when others see me nervous.					

(Continued)

(Continued)

S. No.	Statements	1	2	3	4	5
13	I have clear idea about what I want.					
14	I understand when others like me.					
15	I understand what I am passionate about.					
16	I can understand when others see me happy.					
17	I understand my compatibility with others.					
18	I can understand how others perceive my weakness.					
19	I understand the impact I have on people.					
20	I can understand when others see me with respect.					

Instructions: 1. Transfer the scores of all the odd numbered statements from the table to the ISR column below.

2. Do the same with the even numbered statements to the ESR column below.

3. Total the scores of ISR and ESR column.

Scoring			
Internal Self-awareness (ISR)		External Self-awareness (ESR)	
Question no.		Question no.	
1		2	
3		4	
5		6	
7		8	
9		10	
11		12	
13		14	
15		16	
17		18	
19		20	
Total		Total	

Scoring Details	High/ Low	ISR–ESR	Tick
If ISR greater than 35, then its high.		High–High	
If ISR is less than 35, then its low.		High–Low	
If ESR is greater than 35, then its high.		Low–Low	
If ESR is less than 35, then its low.		Low–High	

own agenda. It's important to remember that we are getting into a vulnerable zone while seeking feedback. One of the effective ways to commence receiving feedback is to seek it from people we trust.

Speak to your closest family member whom you trust (your spouse and children, brothers and sisters). Use the following format for capturing feedback on yourself.

Describe me as a person using not more than 10 keywords.

_____

_____

Explain the keywords with an example or instance (request them to start with positives and then move to development areas).

_____

_____

_____

_____

_____

Think about 'what' made you behave in that manner? What was the impact of the behaviour on others?

_____

_____

What is your key learning from your behaviour for the future?

_____

_____

This exercise can be replicated with the colleagues you trust.

Introspection

The other mechanism to develop self-awareness is introspection. It is the process of self-reflection that leads to understanding the way we think, speak and behave. This needs investment of time in a quiet environment with no distractions. True introspection needs courage, as it might be uncomfortable to revisit some of our emotions and behaviours.

We may tend to avoid stepping into the zone of introspection with honesty. Many may deliberately seek distractions in order to avoid revisiting their unpleasant emotions and behaviours. The human mind is capable, if given the opportunity, of being self-aware with the help of introspection. Unless a conscious effort is initiated through reflection, self-awareness is unlikely to develop.

Introspection Based on 'Why' and 'What'

There is another challenge that we need to overcome in developing self-awareness through the process of introspection. Surprisingly, this provides a comparatively lesser benefit. Research indicates that those who depend only on introspection for examining their own feelings and behaviour were less self-aware. The problem is not with introspection but rather with the method.

The challenge arises when we seek answering the question 'why' during the introspection process. 'Why' is not an effective self-awareness development question. For the question, 'why did I lose my temper with a particular team member', we might not have the answer due to our subconscious thoughts, feelings and motives. We, therefore, become incapable of eliminating those biases while answering the question 'Why'.

We are inherently programmed to think and act in a particular fashion. Hence, the introspection process has a challenge. Let's take an example: 'Why did I lose my temper on John?' The mental response is 'I gave John adequate warnings and had no choice but to lose my temper.' We are enveloped by the defence of justification.

A more effective form of introspection is 'what' rather than 'why'. Questioning 'what triggered the particular behaviour or action' would provide a much better understanding, leading to higher self-awareness.

In a study conducted by psychologists Dr J. Gregory Hixon and Dr William Swann, undergraduates were provided with negative feedback on their sociability, likability and how interesting they are as a person. Some set of students were asked to introspect on 'Why such a feedback was received by them?' The other set of students were asked to introspect on 'What could be the possible reasons for such a feedback?'

The conclusion of the study was that the students who introspected on the basis of the paradigm of 'why' were engaged in justifying and defending themselves. The other group was comparatively more focused on what were 'the reasons for the feedback'. Hence, they were more open to learning from the feedback.

Let's take Sandeep's example.

Sandeep heads the business development department in a technology company. His department had missed achieving revenue targets for two consecutive quarters. When he analysed on 'why' he missed achieving the targets, multiple thoughts were likely to have crossed his mind. He would have attributed the failure to a lack of support from his technical team, lack of skill set in his team and a poor communication strategy.

When he switched over to the question 'what' are the possible reasons, the following thoughts were likely to have crossed his mind—lesser interaction with the technical team, inadequate training for his team on selling skills and his lack of involvement in designing the communication strategy. 'What' generated solution-oriented and more constructive thoughts in his mind. Hence, 'what' was a more effective way to introspect as compared to 'why'.

Sandeep's Story Continues...

Sandeep was a mid-level manager in a large organization. He had seven subordinates, and he was managing a team of 40 members. He was stuck in the middle management level for more than a decade.

Some of the challenges faced by him while handling job assignments were as follows: Sandeep would often procrastinate with the task on hand, and, hence, his team would land up managing the crisis at the last moment. Working closer to the deadline had become a habit with him. When probed by his supervisor, he would justify his habit and not be aware of the consequences of delaying tasks. He would blame everything and everyone else other than himself for the inevitable delays. He often expressed that planning is not an effective method. He believed that completing tasks at the last moment brought out the best in him. Sandeep was not very comfortable in receiving feedback and generally avoided it. On some occasions, he would confess that he was unaware of his weaknesses and was not comfortable talking about them.

What are the key learnings from the behaviour of Sandeep on his ability to introspect?

_____

_____

_____

_____

What would be your suggestions for Sandeep?

_____

_____

_____

_____

What would you:
Stop doing?

_____

Start doing?

_____

Continue doing?

_____

Self-awareness Checklist

Kindly read the statements in the following checklist and add one point for each of the 'YES' and minus one point for each 'NO'. This would provide you with an idea of your standing on the component of self-awareness and help with the development process.

S. No.	Self-awareness Checklist		
	Statements	Yes	No
1	I realise when I am angry.		
2	I can well understand the emotion being experienced.		
3	I realise that I am undergoing stress.		
4	I realise when I am disturbed.		
5	I am not able to think well when I am tensed.		
6	I realise when I am being unreasonable with others.		

S. No.	Statements	Yes	No
7	I believe that being aware of my emotions at any point of time is important.		
8	I well understand when my words and actions impact others.		
9	I am aware when I am tired.		
10	I can understand my state of mind while dealing with people.		

Salient Points

- Self-awareness is the understanding of our thoughts, emotions, feelings, behaviour and strengths through honest and accurate self-assessment.
- Self-awareness has two dimensions: internal self-awareness and external self-awareness, both equally important in building EI.
- Internal self-awareness is observing our own feelings, thoughts and behaviour.
- External self-awareness is our ability to understand how others perceive us.
- Feedback is one of the most effective ways to develop self-awareness.
- Self-introspection on the basis of 'what' rather than 'why' leads to enhanced self-awareness.

5

Self-regulation

In the absence of self-awareness, it is very unlikely that we can move towards the development of self-regulation. If we are not aware of the emotions we experience, it would be rather challenging to regulate them.

Self-regulation is the ability to manage our internal feelings, thoughts and emotions, and to abide by our individual, self-chosen value system. Self-regulation is important in handling our emotions, disappointments and failures. It is the choices we exercise as an individual. It is not about suppressing our emotions and feelings but rather managing them effectively.

When we are exposed to stimulus in our daily lives, we are bound to experience emotions. The manner in which we handle our emotions is driven by self-regulation. It is also the ability to forget, forgive, ignore and postpone our responses rather than react impulsively.

The real need for self-regulation comes into play when we are faced with challenging situations. The mind usually tends to choose the easier route by dispensing with emotions in the overall equation. In laymen's term, we often use the word 'patience' to signify self-regulation. This is a significant component of EI, which leads to effectiveness in all walks of life.

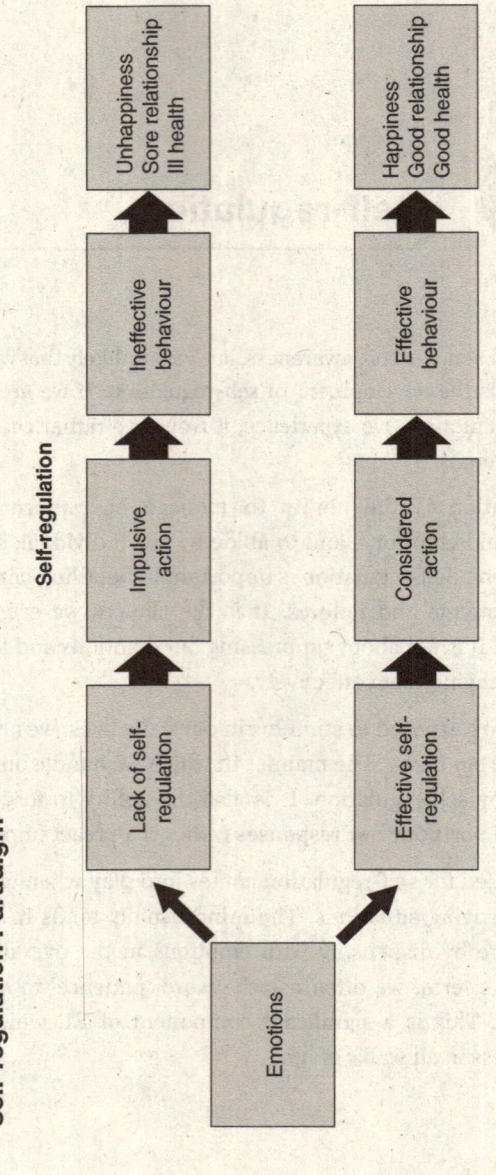

Self-regulation Paradigm

When a sportsman is engaged in a popular sport, witnessed by thousands at a stadium amid a constant deafening noise of cheering and booing from spectators, self-regulation is put to test. If distracted due to unmanaged emotions, it's literally the end of the game for the player. This applies to all walks of life, not just confined to sports.

The ability to submerge our emotions and maintain a steady focus on our goals is the essential outcome of self-regulation. It helps us to manage our thoughts, feelings and behaviour under various situations that we face in our lives.

Self-regulation has two dimensions, namely monitoring and managing emotions. Most behavioural skills are put to test when the going gets tough and things are not in our favour. When emotions take over the executive functions of the brain, they need to be managed well enough to render effective responses.

Our memory and reasoning skills are majorly dysfunctional when engulfed by emotions. Being charged with unmanaged emotions further diminishes our ability to listen effectively. When we are able to regulate our emotions and prevent impulsive actions, we are more likely to be effective in our interactions. The other extreme response is to perennially withdraw from the situation rather than face it.

Self-regulation impacts all other components of EI. It is rather important to understand that our emotions are generated within us and not outside. Hence, the mechanism to regulate them too lies within us. There is no reason to blame anyone but ourselves for our inability to regulate our emotions.

These are some of the early symptoms in children that indicate a lack of self-regulation:

- Children act 'silly' and 'out of control'
- Children throw tantrums and would not subside until they get what they want

- Struggle in transition between activities
- Have difficulty in waiting or taking turns
- Struggle with being in close proximity to others
- Grab, throw or touch things impulsively
- Display of restlessness

These early symptoms can be a wake-up call, making it important to help the child develops effective self-regulation.

Are Emotions Good?

Emotions left alone are not harmful. They are just signals that not only help us to communicate and connect with others but also enable us to understand ourselves better. Each trigger of emotion tells us something. What we do with our emotions is an altogether different proposition.

Managing Emotions

Adarsh faced a lot of anxiety each time he had a presentation with the senior management team. He would get nervous and have sleepless nights. He would forget the key information during his presentation and get stuck. The emotion of anxiety that led to stress was a signal for him to perform well in the presence of the management team.

When he realized that he was under constant anxiety and stress, he chose to prepare himself extensively and had mock presentations in the company of his colleagues. He had to invest more time in preparation, and he gradually disciplined himself. When he realized that the root cause of his stress was fear of failure, he made an extra effort to overcome this fear. In Adarsh's case, his attempt to manage his emotions was constructive. The emotion, in his case, signalled him to perform better.

The other option could have been to succumb to the emotion and start avoiding presentations. He could have chosen to complain, avoid and criticize out of frustration. The choice lies well within each individual in the way emotions are managed.

Rightly said by Dr Steven R. Covey, 'Our life is an outcome of the way we manage our stimulus and the choices we make.' Adarsh started feeling less stressed and, in fact, gradually started enjoying his presentations to the management. This is an example of how well a signal from an emotion was translated and managed.

Self-control

Self-control is overriding our tendency to act impulsively in order to attain an alternative goal. In other words, it is about suppressing diversionary impulses for the sake of achieving the goal. Self-corrective adjustments continuously take place in order to serve our goals. It entails overriding other impulses and diversions. This corrective adjustment originates within the person. It is all about choices.

Self-regulation and Choices

In his autobiographical narration in the book *Man's Search for Meaning*, Austrian Psychiatrist Viktor Frankl highlights the importance of freedom of choice. His point of view is that no matter how challenging the situation is, humans always have the freedom to choose. Making the right choice is determined by how we see the circumstance and create meaning out of it. He calls it the ultimate freedom of a human being. This indicates the ability to make prudent choices in the most difficult situations in life. The ability to make a positive and constructive choice, particularly when we have no control over the circumstances, is the ultimate freedom.

The other option is to be a victim of circumstances, exhibited through behaviour such as blaming, criticizing and complaining. The power of choice ultimately lies well within us. The ability to exercise those choices leads us towards effectiveness.

There are hundreds of stimuli touching our lives each day. With each stimulus we receive, we make choices of responding, reacting or ignoring. The choice is whether or not to let these communications drive our emotions.

Vikas was getting ready for work and he was in a hurry, as he had an important meeting at 9.00 a.m. He was worried about being late due to the morning peak-hour traffic. He hurriedly searched for important documents, which he remembered placing on the table.

After his breakfast, he came up to the table to pick up the documents. He was surprised to find them missing. He searched for them all over the house. His temper grew on him and he yelled at his seven-year-old daughter. 'Nothing can be found in this house,' he shouted angrily. He entered into an argument with his wife on how disorganized the house was. He went up to his daughter and displayed anger for not keeping her room clean.

He hurriedly walked out of the house in anger, slamming the door behind him. He reached the car park only to find that he had forgotten his car keys at home. He called for a taxi and started his journey to his workplace. Due to peak-hour traffic, the taxi was stuck in a traffic jam that made him restless. His anger grew further, as he was getting late for the meeting. Altogether, he had a miserable day with his lingering bad temper.

From this scenario, it can be observed that one emotional spark of anger, caused due to anxiety, had a series of repercussions. The choice of getting angry or not was with Vikas. He caused a chain of emotional outbursts, as it was not managed or regulated well enough. It impacted him and others around all through the day. When emotions are not managed well, it can thus lead to a chain of unpleasant reactions.

Self-regulation is a significant contributor towards being emotionally intelligent. It involves negative thought control. It is like a mental thermostat to maintain a balance of thoughts when faced with an onslaught of emotions.

People with low self-regulation tend to fall prey to addictions such as alcoholism and drugs. This tendency is due to their inability to manage emotional impulses generated because of failure, disappointment and frustration. Strong self-regulation is needed to exercise the choice to keep away from all forms of addictions, including alcohol and drugs. Failure to postpone instant gratification is an intrinsic part of it.

Implementing self-regulation is easier said than done. We humans have a high propensity to act on the basis of our emotions. The combination of understanding our emotions (self-awareness) and subsequently managing our responses makes it challenging.

The compulsion to act, when faced with emotion, is instinctively governed by the amygdala. We need to learn to escape from the amygdala hijack. One of the outcomes of the lack of self-regulation is the inability to take responsibility. We tend to find the problem outside of us and never look inwards. Managing our emotions effectively by turning inwards and looking inside of us leads towards 'emotional freedom'.

More often than not, people find it easy to blame everything and everyone around, rather than looking at themselves. We are often deserted by this component of EI and thereby fail to work on the other components as well. The inability to manage our emotions can become a habit. Considerable effort is required to break free from ineffective behavioural habits in our lives.

We are imprisoned by our habits unconsciously and lead our lives not even being aware of them. Self-regulation helps us to break free from ineffective habits of the past and develop new, emotionally intelligent habits.

Similar to the physical habits created due to muscle memory, mental habits are created in the brain. A repeated way of thinking becomes a habit over a period of time, and we are imprisoned by these mental habits.

Millions of neurons are connected to each other to create a pattern of thinking that in turn leads to behaviour. Physical habits are visible and hence can be understood and dealt with comparative ease. Mental habits, on the other hand, are difficult to understand and act upon.

We unconsciously demonstrate behaviours on the basis of the wiring of our brains. In order to bring about a change in the habit, we must work on its rewiring. Unlike physical habits, rewiring of the brain to change a mental habit takes significant effort. The key to the process of rewiring is repetition.

The best example of the rewiring of mental habits is witnessed in the defence forces across the world. The expected behaviour is drilled a countless number of times as part of their daily routine, which translates into predictable behaviour. Civilian men and women are conditioned to behave in a disciplined and organized fashion through the repetition of actions. The behaviour thus achieved is predictable and consistent.

Emotional Firewall

In the computer language, 'firewall' is termed as a system designed to prevent unauthorized access to a private network. All messages entering or leaving the network intranet must pass through the firewall that examines each message and blocks those that do not meet specified security criteria.

Self-regulation is the emotional firewall for humans. It protects us from the onslaught of emotional meteoric assault on the brain. The firewall is created by striking a balance between rationality and emotions. Emotion is a key dimension in humans, and managing emotions is different from 'being emotional'.

Being emotional is often used in a negative sense. It implies that the person in question has drifted away by the tides of emotions while making a decision. This description is quite valid in a sense. When decisions are made purely on the basis of emotions, devoid of any rationality, they are not effective. The same applies to the contrary.

Emotional Firewall

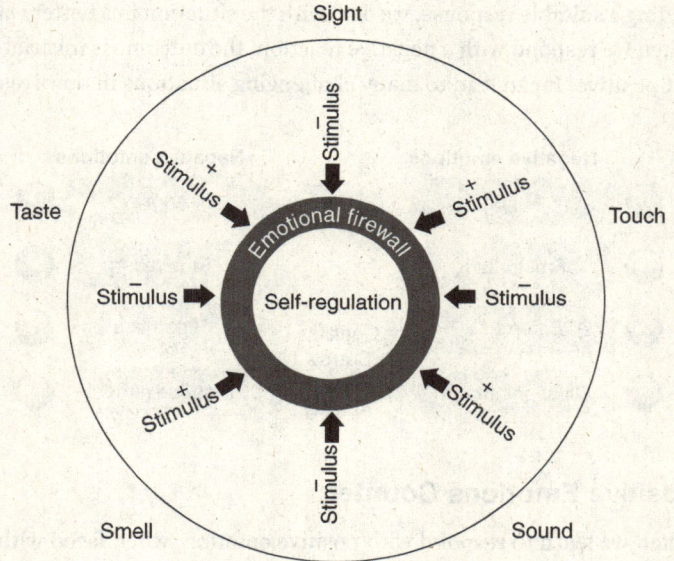

'Emotional firewall' is a method that evaluates all stimuli reaching our sensory organs and regulates them. A stimulus may trigger through senses of sight, touch, speech or smell. It filters unwanted stimulus and regulates messages going into and out of the brain.

The foundation of the 'emotional firewall' is built with the help of strong self-regulation. It insulates us from the negative stimulus, and it also helps us to manage positive stimulus effectively. It is our best insurance against emotional derailment.

Negative Emotional Clash

When interacting with people, if their negative emotions are countered with our own negative emotional reactions, it leads to conflict, sorrow, stress and anxiety for all concerned. We instinctively try to react with emotions similar to the ones we receive. This is a clear indication of the lack of self-regulation.

Once we choose to regulate our instinctive reaction and take time finding a suitable response, we deal with the situation in a better way. When we respond with a negative reaction, the outcome is invariably not positive. It can lead to many challenging situations in our lives.

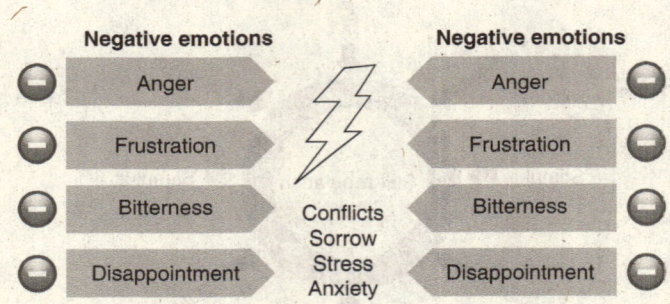

Positive Emotions Counter

When we learn to respond with positive emotion, when faced with a negative one, it changes the whole perspective. This type of response has the propensity to change the source emotion itself in others. We often prescribe this to employees dealing directly with customers in organizations.

When interacting with an angry customer, the recommendation has always been to be calm and respectful. Despite the customer venting all negative emotions, the rule book seeks us to remain calm, apologize and try to solve the problem.

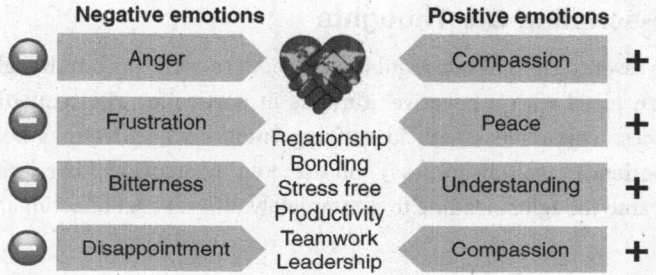

Negative emotions		Positive emotions	
Anger		Compassion	+
Frustration	Relationship	Peace	+
Bitterness	Bonding Stress free Productivity	Understanding	+
Disappointment	Teamwork Leadership	Compassion	+

In most instances, the customer calms down after a few minutes, provided the positive emotion is displayed by the employee. The method in action is to counteract the negative emotion with a positive reaction. After a while, the negative emotion gradually neutralizes. There is a lot at stake while dealing with customers; hence, we are compelled to respond in this manner. Imagine we extend this to other human interactions.

Another effective option in managing negative emotions is to ignore, postpone or regulate our responses. Anger is an emotion that is bound to be triggered under challenging situations. Through effective self-regulation, we can choose to express our anger at the right time, for the right cause, at the right person.

Emotional Clash Exercise

You have been insulted by a friend for whom you have regard and respect. How would you respond to the person in this situation?

- Insult back
- Take a pause and think about the response
- Ignore the incident
- Feel angry
- Show anger on someone else

Re-scripting Our Thoughts

The essential part of self-regulation is about re-scripting our thoughts when faced with a negative stimulus in particular. The regulation process commences with identifying emotions and feelings being experienced (self-awareness) and overcoming emotional barriers to reframe thoughts, leading to a completely different set of actions.

Re-scripting Emotions

Negative Emotion	Imulsive Reactions	Re-scripted Thoughts
Anger I am mad at my boss because he rated my performance poorly.	Complaining, criticizing, showing anger at others, non-cooperation	The onus is on me to establish my credentials, how can I do better?
Anxiety I don't know what will happen to my family if I lose my job.	Being depressed, going into a shell, sleepless nights	What can I do to be more employable? What skill can I acquire, how can I add more value to my profession?
Fear I can't do this well. I shall fail.	Avoiding, procrastinating, blaming others	Can I take help from others? How can I learn to do better?

Postponement of Instant Gratification

A significant study was conducted by psychologists Walter Mischel and Ebbe B. Ebbesen. Children were offered a choice between instant rewards against additional reward if they waited for a while. The reward placed in front of them was a marshmallow sweet. Children between the ages of 4 and 6 were made to sit in a room all alone as part of this experiment.

Participants displayed various self-invented distractions. Some would cover their eyes, others would look away or kick the desk. They were all trying to resist the impulse of consuming the marshmallow. Some children succumbed to the temptation and consumed the marshmallow without waiting.

A follow-up study was conducted 20 years later. It was found that children who waited for a while to get higher rewards performed better in all walks of life as compared to those who could not resist the temptation. Children who waited were socially more competent, self-assertive, managed difficult situations better and had the ability to postpone instant gratification, hence more goal-oriented. It was concluded that there is a distinct relationship between the postponement of instant gratification and success in life. This stems out of self-regulation.

Self-regulation, as a component of EI, was not very popular when this experiment was conducted. This does not prevent us from attributing this experiment to highlight its importance. Impulsive and impetuous behaviour goes against self-regulation. In the past, celluloid characters in popular movies were showcased as 'angry young men' who threw their fists at the slightest temptation and wore their emotions up their sleeves. These characters made a lasting impact in the minds of the audience, and the gate-crashing heroes were role models for many young people. This behaviour is however not tenable in our professional and personal lives.

Postponement of an emotional response is often seen as a sign of weakness. When we hear about successful achievers in any profession, be it sports, business or fine art, the common mantra for success is hard work, focus, dedication, commitment and sacrifice. These traits are a reflection of effective self-regulation. The ability to avoid distracting thoughts and to lay focus on the goal is of paramount importance to reach the pinnacle of success.

It is important to train children at a young age on self-regulation as the absence of it would have a lifelong impact on their effectiveness. Parents need to realize the difference between bribing the child for acting in a particular manner and teaching the child about the benefit of the postponement of instant gratification in order to gain long-term joy and happiness.

Competition Not Good

PayPal co-founder turned investor Peter Thiel encourages people not to compete in his book *Zero to One*. Throughout our lives, it's been drilled into us that in order to succeed, you need to compete.

The other paradigm that will help us get ahead of the pack is to create something new, tread the untrodden path and carve our own space, different from that of competition. By competing, we could get marginally better but by creating our own space, we could be miles ahead and 100x more effective. This profound thought is not only confined to organizational strategy to manage competition but also applies to individuals. From our formative age, we are not encouraged to be creative and to script our own path.

Particularly while dealing with negative stimulus, the common tendency is to compete and confront. The other option is to receive the stimulus, to be aware of the emotions we are experiencing through self-awareness and regularization. Create a unique path rather than dispensing emotions through competing. This is an innovative way to channelize our emotions.

If we compete, we have a good chance of losing, as we could well be competing with the ordinary. At times, people lower your level to match theirs and beat you at their game. Hence, the choice is to elevate yourself to a higher plane to neutralize competition.

Self-control and regulation are controlled by different parts of the brain. Self-control is housed in the medial prefrontal cortex. This is the last part of the brain to develop. Self-control fully develops only by the age of 20–24 years. Self-regulation is what makes self-control possible.

Self-regulation is a mechanism housed in the primitive part of the human brain called hypothalamus. This 15 million-year-old part of the brain controls self-regulation of five domains, namely biological, stress management, emotional, cognitive and social.

The human brain can be divided into three distinct parts:

- *New brain:* Neocortex, 200,000–300,000 years old.
- *Mammalian brain:* Responsible for emotions, care for young ones, amygdala forms this part of the brain.
- *Reptilian brain:* Designed to deal with danger, the human brain alarm system which is never turned off.

Emotional Agility

We normally tend to speak around 16,000 words a day, and we can well imagine the number of unspoken words in our minds. Unspoken words could be either positive or negative. Many of them are entangled with emotions and cannot be openly expressed.

Self-defeating thoughts, for example, could be 'I am not well prepared for this presentation,' 'I shall be able to achieve the targets, but my boss is incompetent' or 'I shall not be able to grow in this company.' The basic human instinct tends to lead us towards negative thoughts. It is natural and nothing unusual. Thoughts laced with criticism, fear and doubt can occur in any healthy mind.

The difference is that effective people do not succumb to or try to suppress their inner thoughts. Instead, they deal with their thoughts in a conscious, value-based, productive manner, which is called emotional agility. In this modern, complex world, it is essential to manage one's thoughts and feelings effectively. Emotional agility helps us to manage stress, minimize challenges and be more creative, which in turn leads to better performance in all walks of life.

This is a critical skill we need to build. Developed from 'Acceptance and Commitment Therapy' offered by psychologist Dr Steven C. Hayes, this skill is designed to recognize patterns, label thoughts and emotions, accept them and act in accordance with our values.

It takes constant practice to be aware and take charge of our emotional responses. Managing emotional responses has three major steps:

- Being aware of the emotions
- Understanding the emotions
- Modifying the responses

In the book *Thinking, Fast and Slow* by Daniel Kahneman, thinking process is divided into two kinds:

- Fast, emotional and intuitive
- Slow, deliberate and logical

Fast, emotional and intuitive thinking has great value under many situations, such as answering questions in an examination in a time-bound manner. However, in situations where emotions are involved, this may be counterproductive. It might be necessary to slow down the thought process, providing time for our responses to reshape our judgement and re-evaluate our thinking.

The process of slowing down does not mean that we delay our responses for a prolonged period of time. The idea is to take time for accepting our emotions and slow down or postpone our reactions. This process gives us the ability to choose a more considered response, rather than rushing with an intuitive reaction.

The human brain has the ability to take account of our experiences and provide an effective response. This can happen only if we allow it by slowing down our responses in emotionally charged situations.

Building Emotional Agility

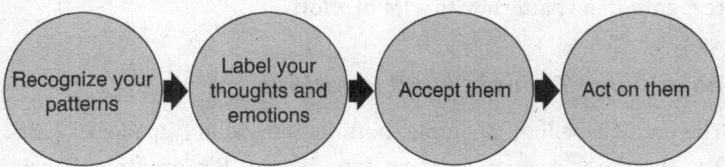

Recognize your patterns → Label your thoughts and emotions → Accept them → Act on them

There are four steps to building emotional agility, namely recognizing patterns, labelling thoughts and emotions, accepting them and acting on values.

Recognize Your Patterns

The first step is to recognize that we are hooked to certain sets of thoughts and feelings. This is challenging, as we could be completely unaware of being imprisoned by them.

One of the major symptoms that help us recognize patterns of thoughts is repetitiveness. These thought patterns return time and again, and eventually become rigid. Thoughts take us back to our experiences, which in turn get stuck in our minds. We must learn how to recognize repetitive thoughts in order to overcome them.

Example: Ganesh failed a few times in his mathematics exam, and his teacher labelled him 'dumb'. When he grew up, he always carried the thought that he can never be good in analytics, for he continued to recall his failure and the remark by his teacher was stuck in his mind. This affected him deeply and he avoided any assignment that involved analytics in his career. He firmly believed that he is not competent enough in this field.

During his school days, he did not enjoy mathematics, as he had no one to coach him on the subject. His teacher's remarks remained as a repetitive thought in his mind, even though he eventually gained a good amount of experience in analytics. The lingering thought that he is not good enough on the subject remained in his mind till he recognized the pattern with a lot of effort.

Label Your Thoughts and Emotions

The act of labelling is simple, nothing but calling 'spade a spade'. Tag the thought as an emotion experienced. For example, 'I have not achieved professional success that I deserve' is the thought resonating frequently in our minds. If so, label this thought. It allows you to observe the thoughts and feelings as they are.

Humans possess the ability to have a bird's eye view of their experiences. Simple mindfulness practice not only helps us overcome these emotions but also makes changes in the brain's cellular level circuitry. In other words, mindfulness helps in rewiring our brain for a new set of thoughts that, in turn, leads to a changed behaviour. If done effectively, negative thoughts would be seen as a passing cloud rather than being fixed and repetitive.

Accept Them

The key is accepting the fact that negative thoughts exist in our minds. They are but natural and occur to everyone. Listen to the thoughts carefully rather than rejecting, hiding, getting upset or being depressed by them. Realize that there are some hidden meanings and messages to these thoughts.

If we take 10 deep breaths, the problem might not be resolved but we would see them in a different perspective. The thought could rather change to 'I have not achieved success professionally as much as I deserve, so what can I do to correct this situation, what are the things in my control I can work upon?' There is a paradigm shift in the thinking process. From a self-defeatist space, our thoughts are redirected to a constructive and positive route. If we fail to work on our negative thoughts, it could be a major dampener throughout our lives.

Act on Your Values

When we intentionally detach ourselves from negative thoughts and emotions, we can expand our choices. We can choose to align ourselves with our values to avoid treading on an unrighteous path.

In the same example of 'I have not achieved success professionally as much as I deserve,' one could use unethical means to achieve success. We run the risk of being ineffective in the long run. The stream of thought flows endlessly into our minds, and emotions change like weather, but values should be firmly rooted in us.

Value Dictionary

W. R. Miller, J. C'de Baca, D. B. Matthews and P. L. Wilbourne of the University of New Mexico drafted a list of personal popular values adopted by people. We need to question ourselves on whether we are aligned to any of these values when we make choices.

Value Dictionary

Accuracy	Duty	Knowledge	Responsibility
Achievement	Family	Leisure	Risk
Authority	Forgiveness	Mastery	Safety
Autonomy	Friendship	Moderation	Self-knowledge
Caring	Fun	Nonconformity	Service
Challenge	Generosity	Openness	Simplicity
Comfort	Growth	Order	Stability
Compassion	Health	Passion	Tolerance
Contribution	Helpfulness	Popularity	Tradition
Cooperation	Integrity	Power	Wealth
Courtesy	Humility	Purpose	
Creativity	Humour	Rationality	
Dependability	Justice	Realism	

If we revisit the same example of the thought in our mind 'I have not achieved success professionally as much as I deserve,' we could make choices such as working honestly, taking responsibility and facing challenges posed by the job. The value at play in this instance would be 'challenge'.

Value Filter

During the process of self-regulation, we are responding to stimulus from the environment. If the component of self-regulation is high, we tend to use the filter of our value system as we respond. With a weak self-regulation, the chances of breaching the 'value filter' is high.

If the stimulus is in control of our emotional responses, we are inclined to breach the value filter. In less challenging situations, we might respond on the basis of our value system, but due to lack of self-regulation, our value system is most likely to be bypassed.

Self-regulation Activity 1: Soccer Team Post-match Meeting

The soccer team has gathered to discuss their performance after losing a match in an important tournament. Let's observe how they are internalizing and self-regulating.

Goalkeeper (John): 'Despite my calling out on many occasions, the backup defence during corner shots was poor. No one was listening to my calls.'

Full back-left (Jaydeep): 'My defence was pretty good. Centre forward missed several chances. They were not able to take advantage of the good passes provided to them.'

Sweeper (Amar): 'Yes, I agree. The problem was with our strikers. They were not quick enough.'

Wide midfield-right (Vineet): 'I think everyone in this room is upset about the loss. We need to overcome our negative feelings, think about the solutions and find a way to win the next match.'

Centre forward (Sandesh): 'The problem was with our defence, the passes provided were not accurate and the ball procession was half in comparison to our competing team.'

Full back-Right (Kumar): 'We did not get enough time to practise before the match. We need to replace the support staff as they are inefficient.'

Captain (Govind): 'I am very upset with all of you. You all were lethargic and good for nothing.'

Coach (Steven): 'I plan to resign from the position, I don't want to discuss this any further.'

Please identify who was demonstrating better self-regulation.

Self-regulation Activity 2

Ganesh, a senior-level executive in a large organization, who was part of the business development team, was presenting performance figures for the quarter. The subject of the discussion was non-achievement of revenue targets for the quarter. Sudeep, the technical head present in the meeting, repeatedly blamed the sales function for non-achievement of target.

Ganesh was pointing out to the challenges faced in the market due to stiff competition, as a result of which there was a revenue shortfall. Ganesh time and again requested Sudeep to wait for his presentation to be completed before analysing the reasons for non-achievement. Sudeep paid no heed to the requests and continued to blame the sales function.

Ganesh was upset by the behaviour of Sudeep and started to get angry. He, however, quickly realized his anger, took a pause, took a deep breath and continued with the presentation. He further realized that it was not the right time and occasion to express his frustration on Sudeep. He recognized that it was due to a feeling of insecurity that Sudeep was behaving in an unreasonable manner.

What are your observations on Ganesh?

What are your key learnings from this scenario?

If faced with such a situation, how would you deal with self-regulation?

Self-regulation Activity 3

Kumar is a finance professional and aspires to move up the ladder in his organization. According to his supervisor, some of his behavioural traits are holding him back, preventing him from progressing in his career.

Kumar often loses his temper on his teammates when things don't go well. This harsh behaviour results in demotivation and many have quit the organization. He is not ready to discuss or analyse problems and mostly blames his team members.

When team members offer suggestions or alternatives, he rejects them with utter disdain. He further believes that people tend to learn on their own. He does not believe in coaching and training his team members.

What are the key learnings from the behaviour of Kumar?

_____

_____

_____

_____

What would be your suggestions to Kumar?

_____

_____

_____

_____

What would you:
Stop doing?

_____

Start doing?

_____

Continue doing?

_____

Self-regulation Checklist

Kindly read the statements in the following checklist. Add one point for each of the 'YES' and minus one point for each 'NO'. This would provide you with your standing on the component of self-regulation and help with the development process.

S. No.	Self-regulation Checklist Statements	Yes	No
1	I can bounce back from bad mood easily.		
2	I am not impulsive by nature.		
3	I can manage my impulses well.		
4	I rarely lose my cool.		
5	I can manage to keep calm in conflict situations.		
6	I can change my mood quickly if I wish to.		
7	I leave behind my professional stress when I go home.		
8	I am generally calm and cool about life.		
9	I can submerge my feelings and emotions when needed.		
10	I can postpone expressing my feelings and opinions until an appropriate opportunity.		

Salient Points

- Self-regulation is the ability to manage our internal thoughts, emotions and feelings on the basis of our value system.
- A major outcome of self-regulation is maintaining focus on our goals.
- Monitoring and managing emotions are two main aspects of self-regulation.

- Self-regulation requires us to rewire our brains through repeated, disciplined practice to form a habit.
- Emotional firewall protects us from the onslaught of emotional triggers through our senses.
- The lack of self-regulation compels us to display negative emotions.
- Self-regulation helps us to respond positively to a negative situation, unleashing the potential to change the source of emotions.
- Postponement of instant gratification is an important component of EI effectiveness.
- Building emotional agility involves four steps, namely recognizing patterns, labelling thoughts, accepting them and acting on values.

6

Self-motivation

S elf-motivation is responsible for driving initiative, enthusiasm, energy, commitment, passion and persistence towards our goals. It is about wearing a positive attitude towards life, thereby impacting our leadership and influencing skills.

Motivation adds flavours of intensity, direction and perseverance in achieving our goals. Self-motivation works magically if our emotions are well directed towards goal achievement.

Emotions are strong drivers of self-motivation. Too much emotional arousal could be detrimental. In the complete absence of emotional arousal, motivation is unlikely to be kindled. It is necessary to find the right balance between emotional arousal and being devoid of emotions, as both extremes are unlikely to lead to effectiveness. In the absence of self-awareness and self-regulation, it is rather challenging to move towards self-motivation. When we are unable to manage the external emotional stimuli and regulate emotions, we tend to drift away from our achievement orientation and drive.

Motivation is not confined to renowned athletes, who constantly push themselves to excel. It is equally applicable to humans in all walks of life. Self-motivated humans have a sense of purpose and propel themselves to greater heights, despite all odds. Self-motivation stems from a high internal locus of control, driven by the inner voice of meaning and purpose. Those with high motivation tend to have a lesser external locus of control. In other words, they need lesser external influence to drive them towards achievement. Optimism too is an important trait of self-motivated people. It is about looking at the positive side of life incidences and pursuing goals despite hindrances. It is the ability to constantly self-recharge, with the desire to achieve and contribute.

Self-motivation is also about choices, for example, the choice to take ownership and move ahead to achieve things even beyond the call of duty. The indicator for lack of self-motivation is being confined to the call of duty and not even fulfilling them effectively. Some men and women are not confined by the boundaries of accountability and strive to achieve more. Self-motivation is prevalent in world-class athletes, as they demonstrate an intrinsic drive to push themselves towards higher goals. Deriving motivation, with the help of only financial goals, is not self-sustaining. For people with EI, self-motivation is driven by passion and a sense of purpose, which is why it is long lasting.

We are motivated to do things that are comparatively easy. Our brain resists taking up challenges and venturing into unknown territory, as it is only concerned with survival. The instinct for survival prevents us from taking risks and trying out new things. Self-motivation works against the gravity of inaction and overcomes resistance of humans in an effort to maintain the status quo. The brain assumes that we have survived with the current status, hence resisting any change.

The primitive man, living in caves, could survive without being attacked by wild animals. Their instinct was to continue living in the caves, as it was a time-tested and proven survival method. It took several millions of years for man to walk out of the caves and settle in the plains. It happened gradually with the advent of the agricultural era.

Evidence of Self-motivation

There are several proofs of self-motivation. It manifests itself in the way we think and act. Each of these evidence needs a closer look, so that we can imbibe and acquire them.

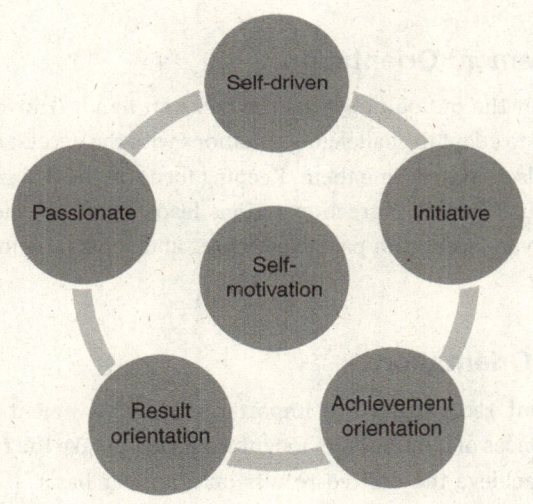

Self-driven

Driven towards goals and targets due to intrinsic drive, it also signifies the pursuance of goals, irrespective of external rewards and recognition. Self-driven people have an internal locus of control and seek pleasure in their accomplishments. External encouragement is not always consistent. Dependence on it may lead to disappointment. Best of results are often achieved by people who are self-driven.

Initiative

It is the ability to seize opportunities on hand by choice. It is about taking charge of the situation to get things done rather than waiting for things to happen on their own or expecting someone else to act. It reflects personal willingness to get the job done. The contra indicator for initiative is lack of action. Initiative also involves the ability to take calculated risks and move ahead despite the possibility of failure.

Achievement Orientation

It is about the outlook towards the tasks on hand. It involves the flexibility to adapt to challenging situations with the necessary energy and mindset to overcome them. Keeping focus on the end result and continuously course correcting actions leads to achievement. It is the ability to learn from past experiences and constantly improving oneself.

Result Orientation

It is about recognizing the importance of achievement and the consequences of failure. The thought is needed to take the necessary steps to achieve the desired results on a regular basis. It involves being proactive and constantly reviewing and course-correcting when things are not going well. It is the focus needed on the outcome through consistent effort. It also involves identifying the best route to achieve the desired results.

Passion

When actions are clubbed with the emotion of love, it turns into passion. When passion drives our actions, financial goals and recognition become secondary. People with a passion for work go the extra mile to deliver the best possible results, not being satisfied with the ordinary. Passion fuels enthusiasm, which in turn generates the energy to drive towards results.

Self-motivation and Execution

Self-motivation is needed for effective execution. Major gaps in execution are not due to a lack of good ideas or strategies. More often, the reason is the lack of execution skills. The ability to get things done is driven by self-motivation. According to Sumantra Ghoshal, execution needs 'energy' on one side and 'focus' on the other. The absence of any one of the two leads to the derailment of the process.

Both focus and energy stem from self-motivation. Focus on the task on hand with no energy (mental and physical) would lead to failure in overcoming obstacles during execution. The contrary is also true. Focus is developed with self-awareness and self-regulation.

Three Layers of Self-motivation

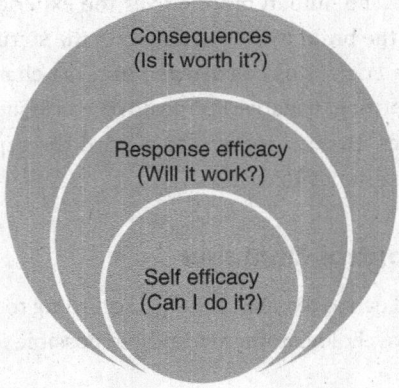

Consequences
(Is it worth it?)

Response efficacy
(Will it work?)

Self efficacy
(Can I do it?)

There are three layers of thought process leading to self-motivation.

Self-efficacy (Can I Do It?)

An affirmative answer to the question 'Can I do it?' will effectively initiate the self-motivation drive. Self-confidence in achieving the goal is the starting point. Failure to address this would make us a non-starter. Confidence in one's own ability comes from self-awareness. Hence, all the components of EI are interconnected and lead to one another.

Response Efficacy (Will It Work?)

A strong self-belief that 'we can make it happen against all odds' is essential. It is the ability to visualize challenges and come up with plans to overcome them. If we are not able to think through them vividly, we would most likely succumb to them.

Consequences (Is It Worth It?)

'Consequence, reward, benefit' factor ensures a strong drive for self-motivation. The human brain craves the experience of reward. Given a choice, the brain wishes to maintain the status quo and save our energy for a crisis. It is constructed to resist change for reasons of survival. A strong negative or positive consequence will drive our minds to act. Hence, we need to reward the reptilian brain to overcome the resistance to change.

Locus of Control Domains

Locus of control drives towards actions. According to E. Scott Geller, a behavioural psychologist, there are three possible locus of control in humans.

'I' (Internal): 'My Results Are Controlled by Me'

When the locus of control is completely internal, the predominant thought is that 'my actions and results are well within my control.' Such a thought arises from the perspective 'even if there are things out of my control, I shall work on them and correct them.' Individuals with high self-regulation operate from the 'I' domain.

Locus of Control Domains

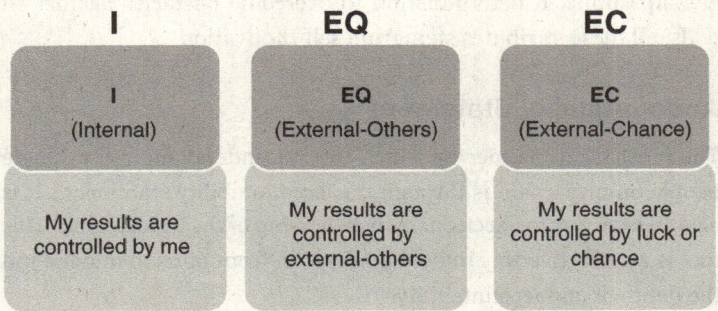

I	EQ	EC
I (Internal)	**EQ** (External-Others)	**EC** (External-Chance)
My results are controlled by me	My results are controlled by external-others	My results are controlled by luck or chance

'EO' (External-Others): 'My Results Are Controlled by External-Others'

Here, the domain is that 'My thoughts and actions are controlled by external factors and people around me.' The belief is that others impact my ability to achieve the desired results as they are not in my control. The stimulus around the individual drives results. Individuals with lower self-regulation would operate from the 'EO' domain.

'EC' (External-Chance): 'My Results Are Controlled by Luck or Chance'

Some operate from the domain of 'My results are determined by luck or chance and we have little or no role to play.' The results are not even dependant on self or the people around but rather left to the happenings of fate and luck. Individuals with very low self-regulation operate from the 'EC' domain.

Self-motivation and Ownership

Ownership stems from self-motivation. The word 'ownership' is derived from the word 'owner'. The individual pursues the goal as he/she owns it. The sense of ownership is further fuelled by achievement orientation. Perseverance in pursuing goals, 'never-give-up' mindset, determination to overcome obstacles against all odds, all these attributes stem from self-motivation.

Accountability Statement

The most lucid manner by which we can understand and evaluate people on ownership is through the 'accountability statement'. It is also an easy way to check our own ownership of the task at hand. This tool is an effective way to hold a mirror in front of us to understand the depth of our accountability.

In a bank statement, we have the credit, debit and balance columns to help us understand financial transactions. Similarly, the accountability statement has details of transactions such as 'what's going well', 'what's not going well' and the end result. It can be illustrated with the help of an accountability statement format.

Goal: Wish to Reduce My Weight by 10 Kg

	Accountability Statement		
	What's Going Well	What's Not Going Well	Results
1			
2			
3			
4			
5			
	Compliment, recognize, credit	Decide, fix, escalate, collaborate, coach, train, moniter	Impact, outcome, achievement

List all the tasks we need to undertake in order to achieve the goal in the statement. Against each of the tasks, list 'what's going well' and 'what's not going well'. In the first column, we compliment, recognize and give credit to the deserving person and ourselves. In the next column, list the tasks that are 'not going well'. On the tasks identified, decide, fix the problem, escalate, train, coach, monitor and collaborate with others to get things done.

When we do the aforementioned exercise, results are bound to come by and we can claim ourselves to be 'accountable'. The same principle is applicable to professional goals as well.

Accountability Exercise

Populate the previous table on the basis of a professional and personal goal to check where you stand on accountability.

Steps towards Motivating 'Self'

These steps are simple and would build the right motivation in us, helping us to develop achievement orientation.

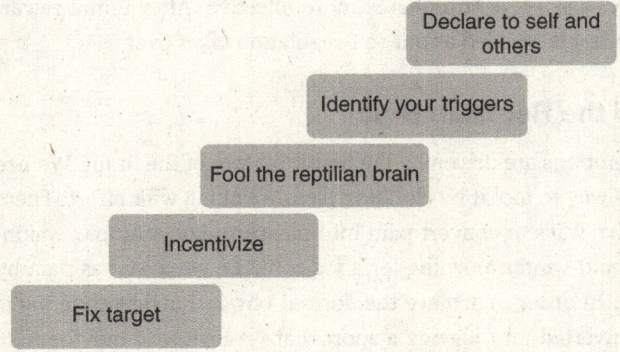

Declare to self and others

Identify your triggers

Fool the reptilian brain

Incentivize

Fix target

Fix Target

In order to move in the direction towards our goals, it is essential to fix targets and milestones. Or else this quote by Dr Steven Covey would be rather pertinent: 'If you don't know where you are going, any road will get you there.' If the target is written down, the goal is better etched in our minds.

It is the constant sight of the North Pole that helps us navigate through the high seas. Most often, wishful thinking occurs in our minds, with no concrete action to back them. If targets and goals are not written down and referred to often, they eventually face a natural death.

Incentivize

In order to achieve our milestones, it is important to incentivize. Human behaviour is driven by pain or pleasure. It is always our endeavour to avoid pain and pursue pleasure. Incentives provide us with pleasure to look forward to, motivating us to strive hard to attain the goal at the earliest. Lack of incentive is one of the reasons why our drive towards achievement orientation diminishes over time. Not in all cases do threats work well enough to make changes in behaviour. At times, it may be counterproductive. It could either lead to burying the head in the ground or get repulsive towards the desired change. Hence, a positive stimulus is more effective. After initial rewards it might not be needed as our self-regulation takes over.

Fool the Reptilian Brain

All emotions are driven by the limbic system of the brain. We need to find a way to fool it by clubbing pleasure along with effort. There are creative ways to convert pain into pleasure. For example, waking up on a cold winter morning for a jog could be perceived as pain by the brain. In order to achieve the desired physical activity, the jog could be converted into playing a sport that we love with our friends. The objective of physical fitness and health is achieved and pain diminishes.

Identify Your Triggers

The trigger towards achievement orientation may differ for each person. It is important to understand the appropriate trigger that works for us individually. If it is blended with passion, it is likely to last longer.

The trigger for Viktor Frankl, as narrated in his book *Man's Search for Meaning*, to survive the Nazi concentration camp under the most inhuman conditions, was the strong desire to not predecease his beloved wife. He imagined lecturing in his college post his release from the concentration camp. This was his trigger to survive, which gave him a strong sense of purpose. Once we identify our sense of purpose, the drive for achievement comes with comparative ease.

Declare to Self and Others

One of the initiatives that will help us to drive towards our goal is to declare our goal to others. This would further propel us towards achievement, as we would not wish to fail in the eyes of others. Our self-esteem is at stake and it appeals to our self-integrity and propels us further.

Self-motivation Activity 1

Sales team meeting post loss of a large client.

Sales executive (Kumar): 'This is a major loss as this client was contributing to 20 per cent of our revenue.'

Key account manager (Kumar): 'There is no way we will achieve our targets this quarter with the loss of this client.'

Sales manager (Yogesh): 'We have a month left for the quarter to end. We can put in our best effort and gain another large account to compensate the loss.'

Sales support executive (Salim): 'Let's find the person responsible for the loss of the client and penalize him/her.'

Pre-sales tele-caller (Robert): 'I have always been saying that we must not rely on a few large clients.'

National sales head (Vivek): 'After hearing all the conversation, I am not sure that we could succeed as a team.'

On the basis of the previous transcript, please identify the leader who demonstrated self-regulation. Think of the reasons.

Self-motivation Activity 2

Sunita was a new entrant to an organization, fresh out of management school. She was not rated well by her supervisor after the first year of work. According to her peers, she demonstrated the following behaviour.

Sunita started blaming and criticizing people around her when faced with failure in her tasks. She found fault with people and refused to accept any mistakes committed by her. She always found problems outside of her when asked to reflect. She often got defensive. Sunita was closed to the idea of finding solutions to problems and rejected suggestions from others.

What are the key learnings from the behaviour of Sunita related to self-motivation?

_____

_____

_____

_____

_____

What would be your suggestions to Sunita?

_____

_____

_____

_____

What would you:
Stop doing?

_____

Start doing?

_____

Continue doing?

_____

Self-motivation Checklist

Kindly read the statements in the following checklist. Add one point for each of the 'YES' and minus one point for each 'NO'. This would provide you with your standing on the component of self-motivation and help with the development process.

S. No.	Self-motivation Checklist Statements	Yes	No
1	I prefer to encourage myself for difficult tasks rather than depending on others.		
2	I can manage my priorities well.		
3	I tend to complete tasks on time.		
4	I am conscious of how I spend my time.		
5	I go after goals once they are frozen.		
6	I like to handle difficult things rather than simpler ones.		
7	I wait patiently to get results for the work done by me.		
8	I believe that work has to be completed as per plan.		
9	I can bounce back quickly when I feel low.		
10	I do better when my inner voice pushes me.		

Salient Points

- Self-motivation is a goal-oriented behaviour with enthusiasm, passion, energy and drive.
- A strong sense of purpose is driven by a high internal locus of control.
- Self-motivation is being self-driven, taking initiative, passion and 'result and achievement' oriented.
- The layers that help in self-motivation are self-efficacy (can I do it?), response efficacy (will it work?) and consequences (is it worth it?).
- Locus of control choices include 'I' (internal; my results are controlled by me), EO (external-others; my results are controlled by external-others) and EC (external chance; my results are controlled by luck or chance).
- Self-motivation drives ownership and accountability.
- Motivating self is about fixing a target, incentivizing and fooling the reptilian brain by clubbing effort with pleasure.
- Declaring our goal to others helps us remain committed to achieve it.

7

Empathy

Understanding Empathy

All humans are born with the ability to empathize in varying degrees. According to Roman Krznaric, author of the book *Empathy: Why It Matters and How to Get It*, our brain is naturally wired to demonstrate empathy. Human evolution would not have been possible in the absence of 'mirror neurons' that enabled people to learn from watching others demonstrate their skills.

Human skills are passed on through generations with the help of mirror neurons in the brain. Empathy comes naturally to the majority of humans. The greatest of social changes in human history has occurred due to empathy, including the abolition of child labour, slavery and many social ills. Economist Richard Layard argues that the cultivation of the instinct of empathy that leads us to care for other people makes us happier.

If we lack self-awareness, self-regulation and self-motivation, it is unlikely that we can empathize with others. If the inner turmoil of emotions is not well managed, it is rather difficult to understand the emotions of other people. It is needless to mention that true empathy helps build relationships and bond with people in our professional and personal lives. When we communicate with true empathy in an emotionally charged situation, it can lead to a transformative experience.

Extrospection

Extrospection is an important tool that will help us to gain empathy. It is the process of examining one's conscious thoughts and feelings. According to Roman Krznaric, focus during the last century has been predominantly on self-help through the process of introspection.

Extrospection is the observing and sensing of what is external to you. It is about looking into the outside world, seeing people, things and nature around with sensitivity. Our sensitivity towards understanding others has to be developed. Extrospection is very important if we have to move from 'individualism' to 'collectivism'. Most of the conflicts stem from individualism and self-interest. Our relationships, happiness and harmony would be enhanced if we develop 'extrospection'.

Channels of Self-awareness

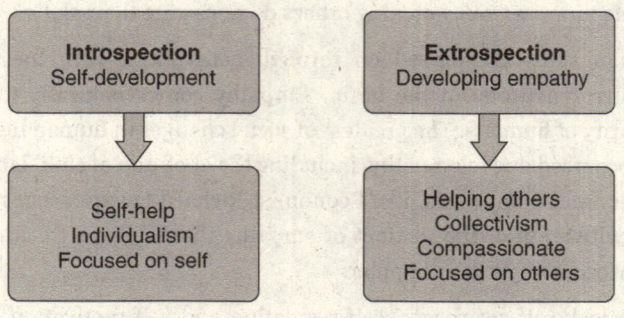

Introspection Self-development	**Extrospection** Developing empathy
Self-help Individualism Focused on self	Helping others Collectivism Compassionate Focused on others

---

Exercise on Introspection and Extrospection

Think of your thoughts and actions yesterday. List all the thoughts you had about yourself, your family and others.

	Thought About Yourself and Your Family	**Thought About Others**
1		
2		
3		
4		
5		
6		
7		
8		
9		
10		

Ratio of Introspection vs Extrospection   I____ : E____

This gives us an indication of whether we are obsessed with 'self' or open for extrospection.

Building Empathy

EI is constructed over a lifetime based on our learning from the environment. Early development of EI is based on our interactions with parents, teachers, relatives and friends.

Empathy Development

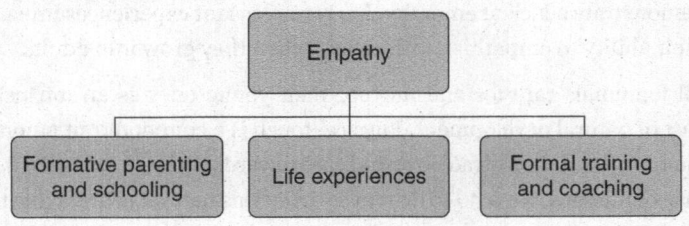

Building EI among children at an early age is important as they are more receptive to learning and absorption. The environment at home plays a significant role in building EI in children. If the family environment is devoid of love, affection and compassion, the development of EI could be stunted. Any behavioural change leads to the rewiring of the neuron circuit in the brain. The upbringing of children in the formative ages, especially at an earlier age, plays a significant role in the building of EI.

Development of empathy in a child is based on the way the child receives stimulus at a young age. If the child receives love, affection and care during the formative ages, the 'mirror neurons' responsible for empathy are better developed. This makes it imperative for parents to pay due attention to the same.

It is often noticed that children exposed to a disturbed family environment, filled with conflict, aggressive behaviour from parents, have diminished empathy, the effects of which become evident in the later stages of their lives. When we observe children brought up in the streets and slums of major cities, devoid of parental love, affection and guidance, we find that they have a higher chance of turning into criminals, devoid of empathy. They are unlikely to be sensitive to the pain of others as they exhibit violence because their mirror neurons responsible for empathy are underdeveloped.

The lack of empathy is not confined to the lower economic strata of society. It is also prevalent among children from economically well-placed families. Children faced with physical or mental abuse may demonstrate a lack of empathy. Early unpleasant experiences impact their ability to empathize with others when they grow into adults.

All mammals care for and nurture their young ones as an intrinsic part of natural development. Physical touch is a common trait among mammals to demonstrate love and care towards their offspring. In the case of humans, we tend to drift away from this natural process due to the compulsions and pressures of modern life. Ineffective parenting and family environment can severely impact the EI of the child.

Other influencers of empathy in a child include parents, grandparents, relatives, teachers and friends. A surprising fact is that a host of subjects are offered by academic intuitions, but hardly any related to right parenting. Young men and women on the verge of entering family life are hardly equipped or educated to raise children. It is left to their conditioned, natural instincts or the process of trial and error.

Empathy and 'Mirror Neurons'

V. S Ramachandran, University of California, known as the Marco Polo of neuroscience, highlighted the importance of 'mirror neurons' in our brains. He pioneered the 'phantom limb' experiment. This research identified the presence of a set of 'mirror neurons' in the human brain attributed to empathy.

The ability of humans to observe a task being performed by someone else and to learn the skills quickly in a matter of minutes is attributed to the presence of certain clusters of neurons termed as 'mirror neurons'. They are called 'mirror neurons' as they mirror the emotions and feelings of other human beings in us.

'Mirror neurons' are triggered when we witness other people experience emotions such as pain, joy and sadness. When we watch a game of soccer and a goal is scored by a player at a critical moment in the match, our 'mirror neurons' momentarily imagine that we have kicked the ball into the goal. At that moment, our legs might actually twitch. These neurons momentarily make us feel exactly the same emotions that we are witnessing. The same is likely to happen when we see other humans demonstrate emotions. It was thus established that 'mirror neurons' are responsible for empathy in human beings. The more developed the 'mirror neurons' are, the more would be empathy.

When we want to develop our musculature, we exercise regularly to achieve the desired result. Similarly, the human brain is developed over a period of time with repeated practice. It is well known that thoughts and actions are triggered by several thousands of neurons connected by a circuit in the brain. There are 100 billion neurons in the human brain. Each neuron makes about 1,000 to 10,000 contacts with other neurons. The permutation and combination of possible connections in the human brain are estimated to be more than the elementary particles in the universe.

The human adult brain is an astounding mystery. With the understanding of neuroplasticity, we can change the circuits in our brain through repeated practice.

Giacomo Rizzolatti, the Italian neurophysiologist discovered 'mirror neurons' in the frontal lobes of the brain. As V. S. Ramachandran further amplifies, the human brain is a lump of flesh, about three pounds in weight, which can be held in the palm of our hands.

Our brain can actually contemplate the vastness of interstellar space, measure infinity, ask questions about the meaning of its own existence and the nature of the creator. It is truly the most fascinating and mysterious piece of work. There are ordinary neurons called 'motor command neurons' located in the frontal lobe, and they are responsible for body motor movements. Each specific physical movement of the body is triggered by a specific set of motor neurons in the frontal lobe. An option is to study the brain of patients who have lesions in some parts, focusing on the impact of these lesions on brain activity and their bodies. Another option is to plant electrodes in different parts of the brain and eavesdrop on its activities and dysfunctions.

Giacomo Rizzolatti performed experiments on monkeys and discovered that motor neurons were triggered when monkeys performed a set of activities. An important deduction from these experiments was that around 20 per cent of the neurons were fired when monkeys saw other monkeys perform an activity. The same set of motor neurons was triggered in the watchers and the ones engaged in the activity. V. S. Ramachandran terms these as the 'empathy neurons'.

'Mirror neurons' are responsible for the learning and advancement of the human race. All development through the ages has been made possible by 'mirror neurons'. It is due to these neurons that we can see a person engaged in an activity and quickly learn and own the same. This is an outstanding discovery, as this establishes the superiority of the human race in comparison to any other species in the world.

As mentioned earlier, children devoid of nurturing and right parenting are likely to have less developed 'mirror neurons'. If they have not received empathy, they find it difficult to demonstrate it. It is the 'mirror neurons' that enable us to put ourselves in other's shoes and feel the emotions.

Empathy Antennae

In order to develop empathy, we need 'emotional antennae'. Unless our brain senses the pain, the agony, the suffering, the disappointment of others, the feeling of empathy may not be triggered. This process is facilitated by the 'mirror neurons'. If the 'emotional antennae' are not strong enough, it fails to catch the emotional signals from others. The sensitivity of the antennae differs from person to person.

Types of Empathy

The core skill in social awareness is empathy. It is about sensing what others are thinking and feeling, even when not expressed in words. We continuously send signals about our feelings through our tone of voice, facial expressions, gestures and numerous other non-verbal communications. However, the ability to read these signals in others varies on the basis of our level of empathy.

Types of Empathy

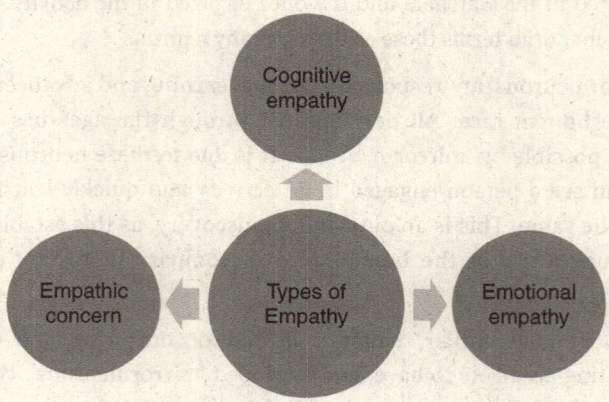

Cognitive Empathy

It is the ability to see things in the way others may think and act, and through which understand their perspective. Leaders with a high level of cognitive empathy inspire their teams to perform better. They understand others, can put forward their ideas with clarity and thereby succeed in communicating well. This influences the motivation level of the team and effectively helps manage diversity.

Emotional Empathy

This trait enables us to feel for others. This is the basis on which we strike a rapport and establish a connection with other humans. Those with a high level of emotional empathy are good counsellors, teachers, client managers and group leaders. They can always sense how others are feeling.

Empathic Concern

This is the ability to sense when people are in need of help. The chances of lending help to others increase with this type of empathy.

People with empathetic concern help others voluntarily. They create good team rapport, which in turn enhances their performance. Empathy is an essential component that leads to compassion, which further helps build EI.

Emotional empathy was studied by Tania Singer, a neuroscientist at Max Planck Institute in Germany. Insula, a fissure that separates the temporal lobe from the parietal and frontal lobes, plays a key role in empathy in humans. It senses signals from all over the body when we empathize with others. Our 'mirror neurons' mimic within us the state of the person experiencing an emotion. The exterior area of insula reads the pattern and tells us the emotional state of the other person.

There are distinct steps towards demonstrating empathy. Understanding these steps would help us practise and be empathetic towards others. Just as for any other skill, repeated practice is a powerful way to develop empathy in us.

Steps towards Empathy

To effectively display empathy, we must understand the four steps that lead us in that direction. A higher form of empathy is compassion, and these steps will help us to develop the same.

Steps towards Empathy

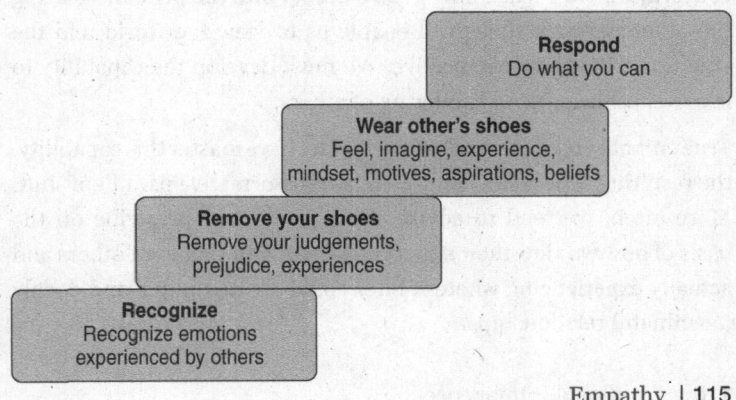

Respond
Do what you can

Wear other's shoes
Feel, imagine, experience, mindset, motives, aspirations, beliefs

Remove your shoes
Remove your judgements, prejudice, experiences

Recognize
Recognize emotions experienced by others

Recognize

The first step is to recognize the emotions of others. It is about having the 'emotional antenna' to receive signals of emotions experienced by people around us. In the absence of an emotional antenna, we may not be able to sense their emotions. With a weak antenna, we tend to either ignore or be unaware of their emotions. Recognition occurs on the basis of verbal and non-verbal cues.

Remove Your Shoes

The common understanding of empathy is expressed as 'putting yourself in someone else's shoes'. On the contrary, the first step towards empathy is 'removing one's shoes'. It is unlikely that we can empathize without removing our shoes. We often tend to be clouded by our own opinions, biases and preconceived notions gained out of previous experiences. We are unable to empathize, being imprisoned by our myopic past experiences that suffocate our imaginations and perceptions. Prejudice and judgement further act as an impediment in understanding and capturing emotions in others.

Wear Other's Shoes

With the help of cognitive, emotional empathy and empathetic concern, we must learn how to dive deeply into the person. Wearing the other person's shoes will enable us to view the world and the situation from their perspective. We must develop the capability to experience the pain and suffering of others.

True empathy is not very easy to cultivate. If we master this capability, the resulting experience can lead to a transformative paradigm shift. More often, we tend to advise, recommend and prescribe on the basis of how we view their situation. Wearing the shoes of others and actually experiencing where it bites could create unique and deeply meaningful relationships.

Respond

Empathy inevitably leads to compassion. A peak of compassion often leads us to a response aimed at relieving pain in others. Thus, the chain of intensity of emotions can be listed as pity, sympathy and empathy followed by compassion. Each of these emotions has varying degrees of utility and effectiveness in our journey towards compassion. When we follow the aforementioned process of empathy, our chances of responding to the needs of others enhance.

Four Steps towards Empathy

Read the short description and relate to the four steps towards empathy.

The environment in the home of the couple Vikrant and Sandhya was not conducive over the last few months. They had been having conflicts with a heated exchange of words, sometimes all through the night. In fact, the arguments were intense to the extent of being abusive. They had not been on talking terms with each other. Moreover, their work kept them away from each other for long durations. Unfortunately their young daughter was often a witness to their conflicts.

One day, their seven-year-old daughter came up hesitantly to the dining table while they were having dinner.

She said in a shaken and fearful voice, 'I am not able to sleep alone, I am scared. I have bad dreams every day.'

At different instances, she expressed her feeling of insecurity in different ways.

'I can't go to school tomorrow as I have not been doing my homework for a month.'

With tears rolling down her cheeks, she said, 'I am having sleepless nights. Are you both going to leave me and go away?'

'I dream of being left alone with no one to take care of me.'

Wiping her tears with both her hands, she said, 'No one loves me in this world. No one talks to me anymore.'

She asked, 'Are you both angry with me? Do you love me?'

Exercise

What is the emotion that you recognize in the little girl?

_____

_____

Did you remove your shoes? What are the perceptions, experiences and judgement you removed?

_____

_____

Did you wear the shoes of the little girl? Did you feel, imagine the mindset, aspirations and thoughts of the child?

_____

_____

What would be your response to the child if you were the parent?

_____

_____

Emotions Leading to Compassion

There are various levels of intensity of emotions leading us towards compassion. Showing compassion is a critical component of developing EI.

Pity

Pity is an emotion that we experience when we see suffering in others. We usually tend to move on with our lives after momentarily experiencing the emotion of pity. For example, we see someone scantily clad, begging for food on the street as we travel in the comfort of our car. We pity the beggar and drive on.

Sympathy

Sympathy is when pity turns into a physical display of concern with the intent of relieving the pain of others. We might not be aware of the struggle experienced by the other person. Sympathy is trying to

Intensity of Emotions towards Compassion

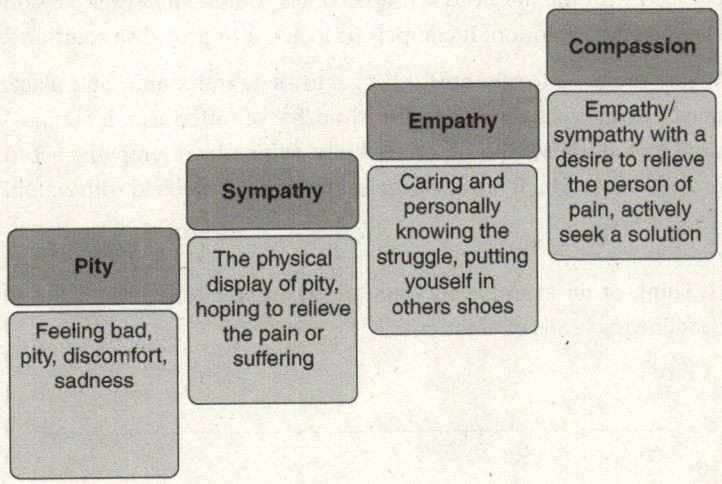

Pity

Feeling bad, pity, discomfort, sadness

Sympathy

The physical display of pity, hoping to relieve the pain or suffering

Empathy

Caring and personally knowing the struggle, putting youself in others shoes

Compassion

Empathy/ sympathy with a desire to relieve the person of pain, actively seek a solution understand the suffering of others. For example, when we get down from the comfort of our car and say a few kind words in order to provide solace to the beggar.

Empathy

Empathy is when we not only sympathize with a few kind words but also display our sympathy physically. We try to understand, to feel the struggle and the painful experience of others. Empathy is deeper than sympathy, as we actually get into the other person. German Psychologist Edward Titchener refers to empathy as *Einfühlung*, which means 'feeling into'. We literally get into the psyche of the other person in order to experience their pain and suffering. For example, when we get into the life of the beggar, deeply experiencing the challenges he/she faces on a day-to-day basis, it leads us towards empathy.

Compassion

Compassion is a higher form of emotion that leads us to act towards relieving the person from pain and suffering. When empathy is clubbed with the intent to act, it becomes compassion. Compassion is not a static emotion. It compels us to act or to provide a solution.

When we choose to relocate the beggar to a safe and comfortable place, maybe to an orphanage and relieve him/her of suffering, it is compassion. Not all those who experience pity, sympathy or empathy act to provide a solution. It is a stronger emotion as it is clubbed with action.

Think of an example in your life when you experienced the following levels of emotions:

Pity

_____

World without Empathy

Imagine a world without empathy. Put yourself in these situations and think of the price we would pay in a world devoid of empathy.

- A child is crying due to hunger and the mother does not respond.
- You are in severe pain in a hospital and the nurse does not bother to attend to you.
- You are too old to walk, but no one bothers to help.
- You are lonely, and no one bothers to talk to you.
- You are lying on the road seriously injured in an accident, and no one bothers to help you.
- You are emotionally disturbed and want to share your feelings with someone, but no one has the time to listen to you.
- You are depressed due to a major disappointment in your career and have no one to console and encourage you.
- You expected your children to be in touch with you in old age, but they abandon you.
- You are financially in a difficult situation and your family members are only concerned with their own demands and comfort.
- You are blind, and no one helps you cross the street.

How would that world be?

What would be your feeling?

Empathy Activity 1

A team member (Sunita) has chosen to resign from her job and the team is discussing the matter.

Marketing manager (Govind): She must be unhappy with her boss, hence this decision.

Finance manager (Samir): She would have landed a better opportunity elsewhere.

Human resources manager (Raghav): We need to speak to her and find out the reason for her decision.

Logistics manager (Nitin): People generally quit for better remunerations.

IT manager (Sudesh): I have nothing to comment on this. This is her personal decision.

On the basis of the aforementioned transcript, please identify the leader who is leaning towards empathy. Provide reasons.

Empathy Activity 2

Ramesh is a technically skilled project manager in a large company. He demonstrates the following behaviour while dealing with people, particularly in emotionally sensitive situations.

Ramesh often fails to observe and understand the body language and facial expressions while interacting with an emotionally disturbed team member. He would not realize this on his own until pointed out explicitly by someone. He is unable to sense emotions in others and prefers logical explanations with facts and figures.

Despite having good intentions towards his team members, Ramesh often fails to connect with them.

What are the key learnings from the behaviour of Ramesh?

_____

_____

_____

What would be your suggestions to Ramesh?

_____

_____

_____

What would you:
Stop doing?

_____

Start doing?

_____

Continue doing?

_____

Empathy Checklist

Kindly read the statements in the following checklist. Add one point for each of the 'YES' and minus one point for each 'NO'. This would provide you with your standing on the component of empathy and help with the development process.

S. No.	Empathy Checklist	Yes	No
	Statements		
1	I can understand other's point of view with ease.		
2	I can avoid being judgemental when understanding people.		
3	I can well imagine the feelings of others.		
4	I can feel the pain faced by others.		
5	I understand why some people don't like.		
6	When faced with a conflict I see that people are different.		
7	I tend to realise when I hurt others.		
8	I know when people around me are disturbed.		
9	I can feel the pain of others easily even when not expressed.		
10	I understand the feelings when others disagree with me.		

Salient Points

- Man is intrinsically empathetic and responsible for some of the greatest social changes in human history.
- Extrospection and introspection help us to develop a deep, sensitive understanding leading to empathy.
- Building empathy in children is an important step towards bringing about their development.
- 'Mirror neurons' help us learn from others. They also help us to respond with sensitivity towards other's pain and suffering.
- There are three types of empathy, namely cognitive, emotional and empathetic concern.

- A strong 'empathy antenna' helps us to receive emotions of others better.
- Four steps towards empathy are recognize, remove your shoes, wear other's shoes and respond.
- Compassion is the strongest emotion in comparison to pity, sympathy and empathy.
- A world without compassion would be unbearable.

8 Social Skills

Nature has designed us more for human interactions than for dealing with machines. The world, however, is heading towards significantly higher human–machine interactions. Human–computer interaction is predicted to be high in the near future. The social human brain is not designed for this kind of experience. The symptoms are already evident. We are losing touch with the skills related to dealing with people.

As we communicate digitally in the form of e-mails, digital platforms and social media, we tend to expend emotions without awareness. For example, when we are angry, we dispense our emotion by typing furiously and clicking the send button. We are unaware of our amygdala taking control over our emotions. This type of behaviour is termed as 'cyber-disinhibition'. The social brain is disconnected when we are not dealing with people in flesh and blood.

This makes social skills important to acquire. It is an intrinsic component of EI that needs to be developed and sustained. Social skills are the nutrition necessary for building and sustaining a healthy society. Absence of this skill can impact our family and social life. It would greatly impact our relationships with the near and dear ones. Social skills constitute components such as influencing, persuasion, interaction skills, leadership and being liked. These skills help us to build effective and strong personal and professional relationships.

It is unlikely that we could develop social skills in the absence of self-awareness, self-regulation, self-motivation and empathy. Unless we are able to manage our 'self' effectively, it is rather challenging to manage others using empathy and social skills.

Social skills are the ability to understand others and the manner in which they would respond to situations. It is also the ability to get along and influence people to cooperate. The ultimate outcome of social skills is to successfully interact with people, manage and adapt to their emotions and exert the necessary influence to get things done.

The traits of social intelligence are as follows:

- Build and value relationships
- Build trust in others
- Possess interpersonal skills
- Collaborate with others
- Develop the ability to understand others
- Be empathetic and compassionate

Social skills help us to receive cues from people and make sense out of them. On the basis of these cues, we choose an appropriate behavioural response, simultaneously evaluating the consequences. Apart from choosing the right response, we must also evaluate the impact it has on others. All of this is interwoven in the form of effective communication.

The nucleus of social skills begins with managing self (self-awareness, self-regulation and self-motivation). These are the components of intrapersonal skills which in turn lead to interpersonal skills or social skills.

Social skills are the catalyst for leading an endearing social life. It is laced with competencies of assertiveness, communication and conflict resolution. People with social skills are liked by others, tend to be less aggressive and are alert to situations around them. Imagine a person whom you consider to be your mentor. When you are faced with a difficult situation, you would most likely reach out to him/her in order to bounce off your thoughts and seek advice. The person whose opinion matters a lot to you must have high EI with effective social skills.

The Case of the Charmer

An organization involved with high-end consulting, based in India, had clients across the world. Consulting involved high-quality, efficient client relationship management. Servicing clients was a joint effort by the back-end research and sales team. On many occasions, when clients were not satisfied with the progress made by the organization, the charmer Sandesh was brought into rescue. He had a great relationship with all the organizational functions and departments and, above all, a persuasive communication skill. He was seldom seen shouting and yelling around, but all the team members would wilfully cooperate with him. His all-round abilities made him the favourite troubleshooter. He would pitch in and charm all stakeholders and solve issues to the satisfaction of customers. He knew when to apply the brake to prevent his emotions from going out of control. Being aware of his thoughts and emotions at all times, he would seamlessly change gears to overcome challenges. He would play by the rule book of communication and effectively steer through in order to get jobs done.

Social skills are not just about being friendly with others. According to Daniel Goleman, it is friendliness with a purpose. It is about developing mutual respect and healthy relationships in order to achieve individual and organizational benefit. Social skills may also be represented as relationship and stakeholder management.

Components of Social Skills

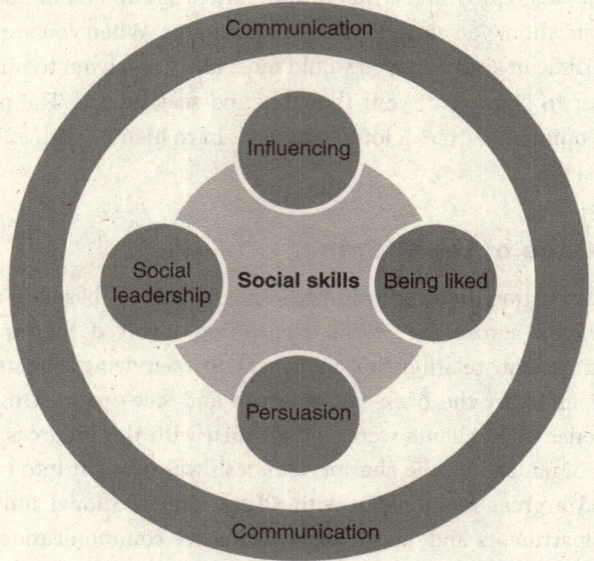

Influencing

Influencing plays a role in helping others to understand and agree to your point of view without commanding, controlling or forcing upon them. When people do not agree with our point of view, influencing skills help us explain to them in a persuasive manner.

This skill requires us to deeply understand the other person's point of view, to modify our communication to align ourselves with their way of thinking. In order to sustain a healthy relationship, it is important to operate under the principle of mutual benefit.

We must be adaptable in order to be socially intelligent. Influencing is more of a dance against the backdrop of give and take. This skill plays a major role in the world of sales, public speaking, politics and many other professions.

Being Liked

In order to develop social skills and build effective relationships, it is important to be liked by others. To achieve the same, we must necessarily understand the perspective of others and modify ourselves suitably.

During a conversation, the focus should be on mutual areas of interest in order to create likability. Particularly when initiating a conversation, it is good to begin with a subject appealing to others around us, rather than being confined to what we wish to talk about. We could always come around to subjects of our preference after we have comfortably established a rapport.

Genuine appreciation and recognition of others help us connect instantly. Many people are obsessed with themselves and their achievements, narrating them mercilessly to the discomfort of others. Once we give equal importance to the interest of people around us, we tend to connect better. The right manners and etiquettes displayed during social interactions make us more likeable. Unless people feel respected, they are unlikely to accept our point of view gracefully.

Persuasion

Persuasion is a well-blended cocktail of rational point of view and emotional feel for the subject. Without either of them, it is hard to be persuasive. More often, it is the emotional component which is missing. Persuasion is displayed through body language, which in turn is generated by genuine intent and integrity of purpose. 'Telling is not persuading, neither is speaking.' Initiating conversations with a pleasing disposition and a warm and enthusiastic smile is half the battle won.

Social Leadership

Being an effective leader in society is significantly more challenging than in a formal organization or institution. Leadership in society is demonstrated devoid of authority or hierarchy with no well-defined roles and responsibilities. The ability to influence thoughts and actions for the attainment of a common goal is no mean achievement. It comes from influencing and interpersonal skills, team building capabilities and being a role model.

Leadership is a social skill as it deals with influencing minds. The essence of a modern leader, in the 21st century, is 'feminine' by trait. Today's leaders, with an ambition to grow professionally and personally, must-have traits such as flexibility, balance, understanding, empathy, humility and openness. All these are termed 'feminine' traits according to John Gerzema, the author of *The Athena Doctrine*. These traits stem from EI replacing traits that were popular in earlier centuries, such as aggressiveness, command and control approach.

Communication

The art of communication is the binding glue for all social skills. Social traits cannot be translated into action in the absence of good communication. Be it influencing, being liked, persuasion or social leadership, none of these can be exercised in the absence of effective communication.

The essential part of communication is listening, body language, tone of voice, facial expression and choice of words. Body language is the fuel that drives effective communication. It is but natural for people to be attracted to good communicators, who effortlessly exercise all components of social skills.

Steps towards Social Interaction

Each interaction is an opportunity to build and nurture a relationship with others. The process of social interaction could be broken into stages for better understanding and demonstration.

Steps towards Social Interactions

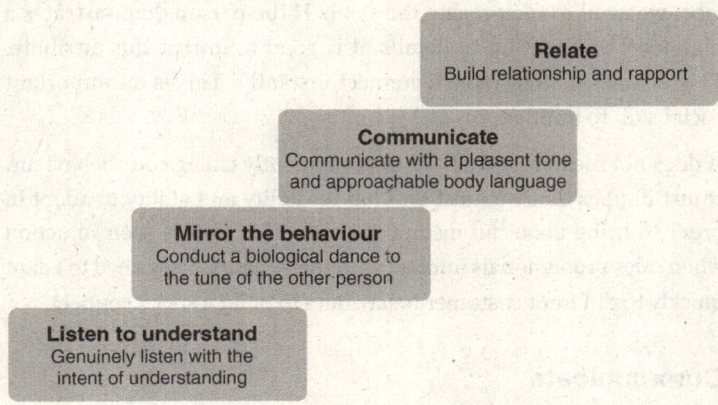

Relate
Build relationship and rapport

Communicate
Communicate with a pleasant tone and approachable body language

Mirror the behaviour
Conduct a biological dance to the tune of the other person

Listen to understand
Genuinely listen with the intent of understanding

Listen to Understand

The first step towards social interaction is to listen with genuine intent in order to understand. Listening is the component commonly missing in social skills. The ability to listen to other people without interruption, offering advice and prescribe remedies only after deeply understanding their situation and point of view plays a major role. As Dr Stephen Covey puts it, 'the one who listens does more work.' Without a doubt, listening is the first step towards building social interaction.

Mirror the Behaviour

This is a form of psychological dance performed to build relationships. The method is to adapt to the behaviour of the person we are interacting with. The trick is to mirror their behaviour in order to win their interest. The premise in action here is that people love their own behaviour, which has helped them with their achievements so far.

For instance, if the person we are interacting with sends a friendly vibe, we need to reciprocate the same. If the person demonstrates a high level of attention to details, it is good to mirror this attribute. This enables us to establish connect instantly. This is an important social skill to imbibe.

It does not mean that we have to permanently change our behaviour. It just implies that we must develop flexibility and ability to adapt in order to bring about an instant connect. This trait is seen in action when sales professionals interact with their clients. They need to adapt quickly to different customer behaviours to build a social connect.

Communicate

The importance of communication has been highlighted earlier. Once the initial rapport is established with listening and mirroring behaviour, effective communication takes the interaction to a higher plane. If either listening skill or the ability to express oneself is not good enough, it creates an impediment in building social relationships.

Relate

The ultimate aim of social skills is to build rapport with people. It is important to relate to the needs and wishes of the person we are interacting with. Once we establish trust and rapport, it paves the way for building strong relationships. A socially educated person operates purely on the principle of give and take. Social skills, built only with the intent of driving self-interest, cannot be sustained in the long run. All successful social relationships operate under the paradigm of mutual benefit.

Levels of Social Interaction

During social interactions, we tend to build relationships in stages. Levels of interactions are involved in the process that starts with

Levels of Social Interaction

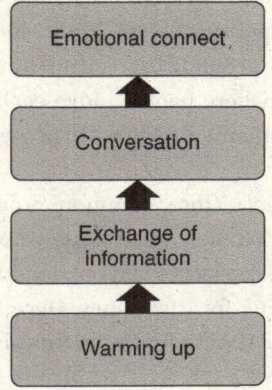

being a stranger and concludes with achieving an effective social connect. This often can be witnessed when we interact with unknown people at the airport or any other public space. In social interactions, gaining mutual comfort happens gradually. The levels of social interaction are as follows:

- *Warming up:* Conversations initially start with an exchange of greetings and pleasantries. It begins with small talk and general enquiries among people and gradually expands to subjects of mutual interest.
- *Exchange of information:* Subsequent to the exchange of pleasantries, the interaction graduates to sharing of information. This stage emerges once the initial comfort and trust are established. The interaction tries to find a common ground based on the information shared. This enables further progress towards strengthening the relationship.
- *Conversation:* Sharing of information further leads to conversation based on the information shared about each other. At this stage, mutual interest and common points of view, likes and

dislikes are established. Exchange of opinions becomes more liberal and those who are interacting tend to agree and disagree freely on various points of view. At this juncture, if they do not strike a common ground, the conversation most likely ends. This is the stage where people judge each other. Their judgement determines their willingness to proceed further or end the interaction.

- *Emotional connect:* Once common ground is achieved, an emotional connect commences. Those who are interacting start sharing personal experiences and opinions, develop an emotional connect and a liking for each other. Once this stage is reached, there is a very good chance for the relationship to continue.

Tips for Social Skills
The Challenge of Being an 'I' Specialist

People whose focus is on the 'self' and 'I' are the 'I' specialists. With a self-centred approach, 'I' specialists create a distinct barrier in building social relationships. Those who are obsessed with 'I' syndrome are seldom popular in social circles and are generally avoided. No one wants to listen to people blowing their own trumpets.

'I' specialists are generally insecure about themselves due to lack of self-awareness and reduced self-esteem. They have the obsessive need to talk loudly about their achievements, irrespective of people's interest. This has to be avoided by those wishing to master the skill of building effective social relationships. It is about timely 'self-disclosure' which is nothing but understanding exactly when to disclose personal information and attainments.

Tolerance towards Dislike

Be it people, food, things or environment, tolerance is an important trait that is needed for being socially intelligent. We might dislike many things around us. It is, however, very important to ignore or accept shortcomings in others, depending on the situation. We must recognize positive aspects in people that will facilitate the building of social skills. Those with strong likes, dislikes and preferences do not connect with others easily.

Use of Humour

The two dimensions of humour are receiving humour gracefully and using humour appropriately. At times, people are good at using humour but not sportive enough to receive the same. Humour is a potent weapon not only to dilute tense situations but also to build comfort and rapport with people around. Self-depreciating humour is often an effective way to build approachability. Of course misplaced and untimely humour is counterproductive.

Being Helpful

Offering a helping hand when others are in need lays a strong foundation in building relationships. If done with no expectation, the act of helping gains more significance and recognition. Most of the times, small gestures go a long way in developing a strong bond with one another. Rendering help to those in need builds a strong emotional connect with people.

Being Inclusive

It is important to connect to a larger number of people in social gatherings, rather than being confined to a few known people with whom we are comfortable. Instead of creating small groups for interaction, we must be inclusive. Meeting and interacting with new, unfamiliar faces is necessary for achieving more acceptability in social circles.

Social Human

Imbibing the traits of a social human goes a long way in helping us to achieve success in our lives. Some of the important social human traits that help us build relationships and networks are as follows: thinking of mutual benefit, understanding group dynamics, handling conflicts effectively, persuasive communication, walking the extra mile with people, empathizing with others and willing to celebrate.

Due to the onslaught of technology, we are debilitated in some of the aforementioned traits. In order to effectively demonstrate the social human in us, we need to consciously learn, practise and develop these traits.

Dimensions of Social Skills

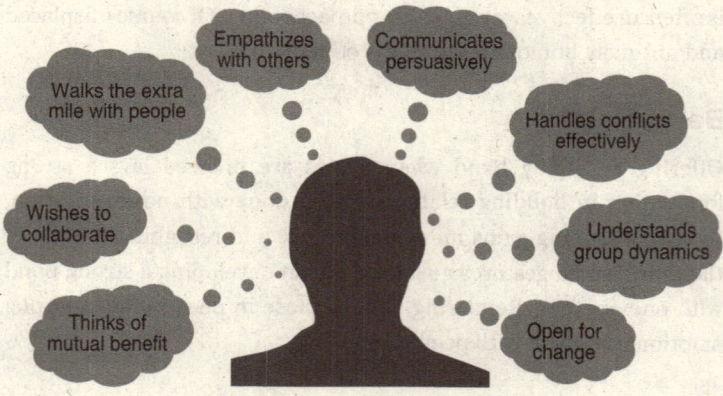

Social Skills Activity 1

A group of friends is discussing in a social gathering.

Ramesh: I feel that we are confined to our group. We should move around and interact with others in the gathering.

Kapil: Let's continue among us as we are having a good time.

Rohit: We can discuss freely in this group. I am not sure whether we will be able to do the same with others in the gathering.

Sarosh: I agree. It is good to have some privacy.

Sudha: I am happy to be left alone. Whoever interested can come and connect with me.

Geeta: Each time I try interacting with unknown people, I land up having a conflict with them.

On the basis of the previous transcript, please identify the person who demonstrated social skills. Think of the reasons.

Social Skills Activity 2

Geeta works in the training function of a large corporation. Most of the time, she fails to get things done when given the opportunity. Her supervisor has the following observations on her behaviour.

Geeta often hesitates to interact with people from other functions. She lacks the skill of persuading others, hence she fails in getting jobs done. Geeta tends to avoid unfamiliar people as she is comfortable interacting with people known and familiar to her. She often enters into conflict with people and is unable to resolve them.

What are the key learnings from the behaviour of Geeta?

_____

_____

_____

_____

What would be your suggestions to Geeta?

_____

_____

_____

_____

What would you:

Stop doing?

_____

_____

_____

_____

Start doing?

_____

_____

_____

_____

Continue doing?

_____

_____

_____

_____

Social Skills Checklist

Kindly read the statements in the following checklist. Add one point for each of the 'YES' and minus one point for each 'NO'. This would provide you with your standing on the component of social skills and help you with the development process.

S. No.	Social Skills Checklist		
	Statements	Yes	No
1	I listen before I respond.		
2	I can influence people easily.		
3	I get along with people comfortably.		
4	I prefer to work with various teams.		
5	I adapt to changes comfortably.		
6	I understand the dynamics of a group well.		
7	I am keen that others should be happy in my company.		
8	I like to work in teams and build relationships.		
9	I am good at resolving conflicts among people.		
10	I can communicate effectively to the understanding of others.		

Salient Points

- Building social skills is important as we are designed more for human interactions rather than with machines.
- Technological advancement has led to increased human to machine interactions, leaving us wanting in the area of social skills.
- Acquiring social skills offers competencies such as the ability to influence, assertiveness, communicate effectively and resolve conflicts.
- Social skills allow us to be persuasive and be liked by others.
- Listening with genuine intent, mirroring behaviour, communicating with clarity and building a good rapport with people are vital social interaction skills.

- Social interaction starts with 'warm-up' conversation and moves on to the exchange of information and personal details before establishing an emotional connect.
- Focusing on others, rather than being an 'I' specialist. Tolerance towards dislike, use of humour, being helpful and inclusive are tips for improving social skills.

9

Building and Driving EI

In the field of EI, there is a definite vacuum. More emphasis is being placed on the understanding of 'why' EI is needed and 'what' is EI. A significant part of 'how' to develop EI has received competitively lesser attention. The subject of building and driving EI is not offered the necessary importance in our education system, as well as in corporate training.

Contrary to IQ, EI can be built at any stage and at any age. This does not mean we have to wait till our ripe age. The process of developing EI involves building EI components and driving EI, which are dealt with in detail in this chapter.

Leading an Emotionally Intelligent Life

Building emotional intelligence

1. Mindfulness
2. Resilience
3. Compassion

Leading emotionally intelligent life

Driving emotional intelligence

1. Break
2. Mirrors
3. Gears
4. Rules
5. Steer

We need to address EI learning to the limbic brain. Unless we are emotionally committed to the development of this intelligence, we may not be motivated to invest enough effort. With age, the EI component is likely to improve. But we can hasten the process of learning with the help of training and coaching. The earlier we commence the learning journey, the more beneficial it would be for us.

A common belief in the past was that the human brain is born with a huge amount of brain cells, gradually lost over our lifetime. New understanding of the brain is based on the effect called 'neurogenesis'.

It is believed that each day, the brain generates 10,000 stem cells, which split into two parts. One part becomes a daughter line and continues making stem cells, and the other part takes various forms in the brain structure. Over a short period of time, the new cells create 10,000 new connections with other cells to form new circuitry.

Neurogenesis adds to our understanding of neuroplasticity. Brain plasticity is the ability of the brain to continuously change and adapt, based on our learning and life experiences. The neuron circuitry can be modified with a conscious effort by changing our thoughts, feelings and emotions. EI is one such ability that can be achieved through conscious effort.

There are two significant components to developing EI, namely 'building EI' and 'driving EI'. The first component can be achieved through mindfulness, resilience and compassion. The second can be achieved by following these steps: brake, look into the mirrors, change gears, respect rules and power steer. Building EI involves gathering emotional fuel, which helps in 'driving EI'.

Building EI

The necessary foundation for building EI is based on three main components. Continuous investment in these areas would provide guaranteed results. It is necessary to work on all three components in order to see sustained results in managing our emotions better. The recipe for lifelong health, good relationships, professional and personal success and happiness lies in the effective implementation of these components.

Building EI

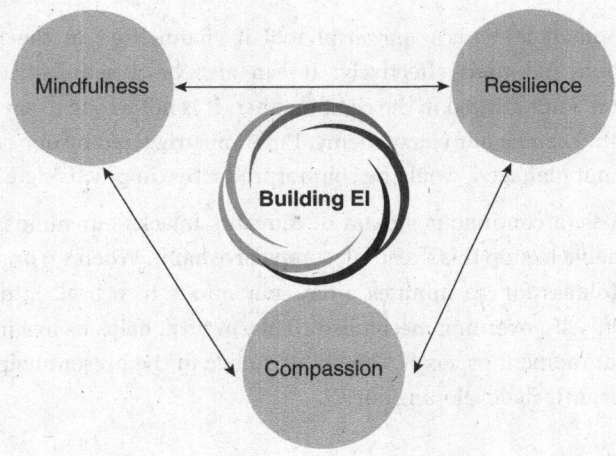

Mindfulness

Mindfulness is being in the present moment. It is about eliminating thoughts related to the problems, challenges and misfortunes of the past and the concerns, worries and uncertainties of the future. It is a state of mind that focuses on the present, feels and enjoys the surrounding environment.

Mindfulness is about experiencing people, situations and nature in the present moment. It is also about building consciousness and a feel for our surroundings. Mindfulness is the first step towards becoming emotionally intelligent. This is the fundamental step, and it is comparatively more challenging to practise.

In the book *Power of Now*, Eckhart Tolle describes mindfulness as follows:

> Being not only beyond but also deep within every form, as it's the innermost, invisible and indestructible essence. This means that it is accessible to you, know your deepest self, your true nature. But don't seek to grasp it with your hand. Don't try to understand it.

The human mind is a powerful tool if channelized in the right direction and used effectively. It can also be a self-destructive weapon if not utilized in the right manner. It is not wrong to say that our mind can be our worst enemy. Emotions triggered by our mind, when not managed, would be counterproductive in practising EI.

At times, a continuous stream of thoughts hijacks our minds. We are unable to stop this dreadful, compulsive habit. When we practise mindfulness for 30 minutes a day, our minds turn back into our inbuilt, self-governing mechanism. This, in turn, helps us live in the present moment or 'now'. The ability to live in the present helps us significantly in developing our EI.

Building EI through Mindfulness

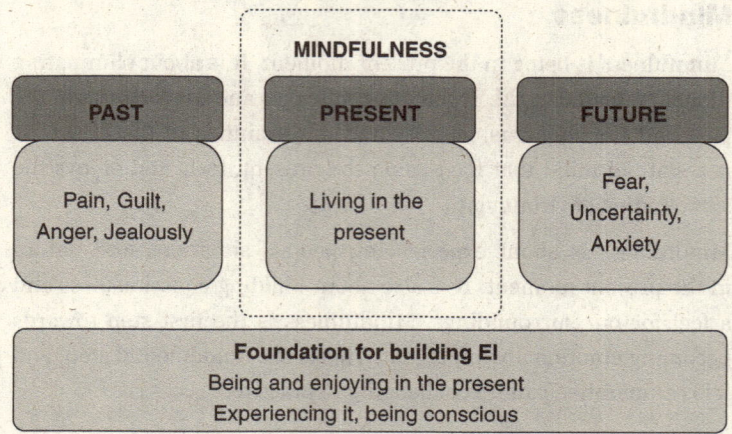

Be the Witness of Your Thoughts

The special ability to witness our thoughts as a stranger will enable us to manage emotions better. It will help us to detach from the emotions, thereby allowing us to handle them with clarity. Human beings are the only ones capable of being 'self-aware'. In other words, we have the ability to visualize our thoughts by being an external witness to ourselves.

This ability can be put to use to make our lives easier through better management of emotions. The only way to improve self-awareness is through knowing and understanding ourselves. Mindfulness is a spiritual experience that helps to build all the required components of EI.

Fear in Our Minds

The human mind constantly perceives threats of the future, which is the basis of fear and insecurity. Fear manifests itself in the form of unease, worry, anxiety, nervousness, tension, phobia, etc. Fear is mostly about something that might happen in the future.

Lucius Annaeus Seneca, the ancient Roman philosopher, in his *Letters from a Stoic* says, 'If you really want to escape the things that harass you, what you're needing is not to be in a different place but to be a different person.'

Uncertainty of the future is the most common worry and anxiety affecting humans from time immemorial. The intensity and diversity of worry have multiplied in the 21st century and is likely to increase in times to come.

The complexity of our professional and personal lives is growing leading to more anxiety about the future. At one end, technology has brought us comfort, productivity, efficiency and convenience. But our lives have shifted to the fast track with increased complexity and change. This has resulted in enhanced stress, making it very important for us to learn how to manage our emotions better.

Perfection Syndrome

Many of us tend to set a benchmark of perfection in different walks of life. The attempt towards perfection is driven by external factors such as comparison, competition, jealousy and the need to live up to the expectations of others and the influence of role models.

Perfection is impossible and it should not be attempted. On the other hand, what is possible is transformation. We have the opportunity to change, learn and grow, irrespective of our background and circumstances. Mindfulness is one of the most effective ways to transform ourselves.

Mindfulness and Happiness

Being present in the current moment during mindfulness meditation is not easy. Mind repeatedly compels us to wander into the past and the future. According to Harvard psychologists Matthew Killingsworth and Daniel T. Gilbert, a wandering mind is not a happy mind. Our minds wander for the most part of the day, delving on aspects that actually matter the least to us. Literally, half of our lives are consumed by such obsessive thinking. They further say that 'The ability to think about what is not happening is a cognitive achievement that comes at our emotional cost.' Unlike other animals, the human mind invests significant energy in contemplating events that have either happened in the past or are likely to happen in the future.

Mind-wandering appears to be the human brain's default mode of operation. It is well established that wandering of the mind is the root cause of unhappiness, according to Matthew Killingsworth in 'The Future of Happiness Research'. Mindfulness is about training our minds to focus on the 'here and now'.

Mindfulness can be attained by 'activity-dependent plasticity'. This is a function by which the brain is continuously modified. About 150 trillion cell-to-cell communication occurs in the human brain in response to everyday experiences and stimulus. This happens without the involvement of the neocortex, which is responsible for rational behaviour. It is essentially the survival mechanism of the brain designed to relate to past experiences and future uncertainties in order to initiate appropriate actions.

During meditation, areas of the brain showing activity are the ones responsible for focus and attention. These areas include the prefrontal cortex, visual cortex, superior frontal sulcus, supplementary motor area and intraparietal sulcus.

Areas of the brain that get active when we demonstrate empathy are the insula, the somatosensory cortex and the anterior cingulate cortex. Meditation calms the mind, reduces stress levels and reduces the secretion of the stress hormone cortisol. Evidence indicates that meditation enhances the immune system of the body.

> Mindfulness is the thin edge of a wedge that, if inserted deeply enough into our minds, will open them to wisdom.
>
> —Andrew Olendzki, Buddhist scholar

Wisdom is different from awareness. It is the knowledge and good judgement gained from life experiences.

Awareness and wisdom will work together once we start practising mindfulness. During the process of mindfulness meditation, emotions such as anger, sadness and anxiety are bound to come up and must be allowed to pass through. Not being consumed by these emotions will minimize our impulse to act.

Many people derive a sense of peace and calm from activities such as painting, cooking, carpentry, dancing and reading. It is true that these activities provide us with peace of mind on a temporary basis. Mindfulness meditation leads to enhanced consciousness and provides us with superior peace, tranquillity and happiness in the long term.

There are various forms of meditation that we can choose from such as yoga, transcendental meditation and mindfulness meditation. We can settle for an apt meditation practice that offers us the best results. In this book, we focus on mindfulness meditation as it can be done anywhere at any time of the day.

Happiness is the destination we all strive to reach. Mindfulness teaches us how to live and enjoy every single moment and thereby derive happiness. We can learn how to create moments of joy, and an overall feeling of happiness, as many times as we wish in a day by practising the mindfulness exercise.

Dr Neal E. Miller, an American psychologist, researched on the autonomous nervous system. What was believed to be uncontrollable, such as the rate of heartbeat and the amount of blood flow in the circulatory system, can actually be controlled. Mindfulness and other forms of meditation play a role in regulating our oxygen consumption and metabolism.

The best benefits are derived when we enjoy the mindfulness exercise and make it an intrinsic part of our lives rather than perceiving it as a painful activity. Mindfulness exercise requires us to stop talking, both externally and internally. When done in utter silence, it offers immense benefits.

Steps towards Mindfulness Meditation

The steps towards mindfulness meditation are as follows.

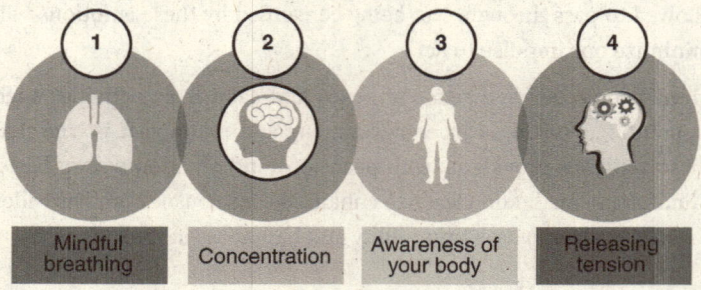

Mindful Breathing

The first step is to focus on our breath. This involves noticing the continuous repetition of 'breathing in' and 'breathing out', making us conscious of the breathing process. Visualize the air going into the body, through the nose into the lungs, and visualize the reverse process as we breathe out.

When we are fully focused on breathing, all our thoughts are completely cut off. Initially, there would be a lot of intrusive thoughts from the past and the future attempting to invade and hijack our minds. With persistence and practice, we can attain total focus on the breathing process.

 Concentration

While 'breathing in' and 'breathing out', be completely attentive to the process. Mindfulness stays as long as we focus on our breath. The idea is to keep noticing the breathing process with a single-minded focus, irrespective of how long or short the breath is. This improves the quality of mindfulness and enhances our concentration.

When we do this diligently, unwanted thoughts gradually reduce and eventually stop. Distractions are eliminated over a period of time. A sense of harmony and peace sets in. Over time, the mindfulness exercise becomes effortless. This needs focused practice initially before it becomes a habit to preserve.

 Awareness of Your Body

Once we have managed to concentrate on our breath, we then need to turn our attention to the body. This means that we have to recognize the existence of the body, making it a reality in our consciousness.

If we notice, our body and mind are mostly disconnected. We are unable to be conscious of our physical existence unless we are hurt or suffer from some kind of physical pain. When the body and mind are seamlessly synchronized, we become truly alive.

We are then conscious of the wonderful world around us. We start living in the 'now' rather than in the past and the future. This is in stark contrast to the lives that we lead presently with a constantly wandering mind, devoid of consciousness. In order to build consciousness of our body, we need to notice every single part from toe to head, deeply visualizing the functioning of the organs.

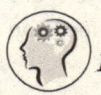 ### *Releasing Tension*

The next step is to release tension and pain accumulated in the body over a period of time. Our mind so far has not been linked to tension and pain, hence the suffering. It is important to learn how to release tensions and free ourselves from psychological and physical pain.

We are conditioned to build unnecessary stress and anxiety. For example, when we wait in a queue for long, stress and tension start building. Similarly, while driving in a hurry to reach the destination, if we have to wait at the red signal, we tend to become anxious.

We must consciously convert such situations into opportunities. Mindfully practising breathing in and out, and focusing on the body helps release stress. In other words, use the waiting time as an opportunity to practise mindfulness rather than being consumed by tension.

Apart from the sitting meditation, 'walking meditation' is also a powerful tool. Mindfulness can be practised in the form of 'walking meditation' as well as using the same principle of 'being in the present'.

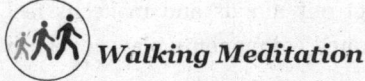 *Walking Meditation*

The effects of walking meditation last longer than that of sitting meditation. Walking meditation enables us to walk long distances with ease, apart from aiding with digestion. Mindful walking has to be done slowly, being completely aware of each and every movement.

The method is as follows:

- Keep your feet together.
- Tie your hands behind you and be in an upright position.
- Place your right foot one foot ahead of your left foot.
- While doing so, say 'right' (should be done while placing the foot, not before or after).
- Then repeat this with the left foot.
- Reach the end of the path and stand there. Say 'I am standing.'
- When you want to turn around, do it in two stages. Place your right foot at a 90° angle and join the left foot. Call out 'I am turning.'
- When you reach the other end of the path, repeat the process.
- If your mind wanders, stop, stand still and say 'I am thinking about...'
- The whole exercise needs to be done slowly, with complete consciousness of every step of your walk.

There are other yogic practices, such as *pranayama*, which are immensely effective. Breathing and walking practices help to calm the mind and minimize the wandering of the mind.

Resilience

Resilience is the second component of building EI. The manner in which we treat our body has a profound impact on our EI. We notice that disturbed sleep, unhealthy food and sedentary lifestyle devoid of physical activity impact our moods and make us feel irritated. Each of the aforementioned components plays a role in our emotional health.

Meditation (Mental Gym)

Mindfulness exercise, both sitting and walking, must become an intrinsic part of our lives. This activity can be viewed in terms of building our psychological health in the form of 'mental gym', just like our visit to the gym for physical body workout.

El Fuel

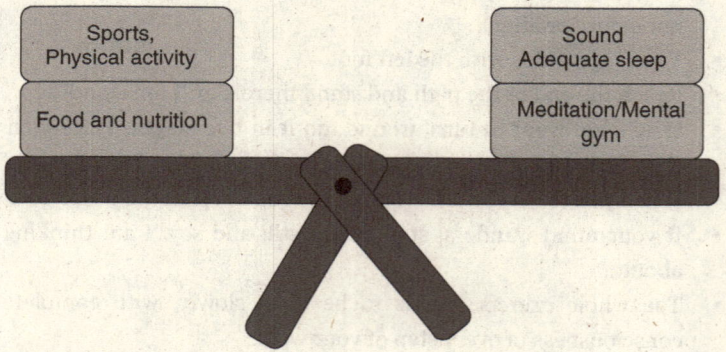

Sports and Physical Activity

Sporting and physical activity work in four different ways.

Heart

With physical activity, our heart beats faster and pumps more oxygen-rich blood. Oxygen-rich blood, in turn, energizes the brain, making it more effective, helping us to manage our moods.

Neurons

Exercise stimulates the brain to produce new brain cells. Contrary to the earlier belief, new neurons can be produced by the exercise of the body. Exercise also helps with developing 'neuroplasticity'.

Physical activities help by repairing damaged brain cells, keeping them healthy. The overall health of the brain improves. Evidence shows that the deterioration of the brain cells can be reversed with the help of regular exercises. Fat deposits around brain cells can be dissolved, and this helps the brain to function better.

Reduces Stress

In response to stress, the level of various hormones in the body changes. Reaction to stress is associated with enhanced secretion of a number of hormones, such as glucocorticoids, catecholamine, growth hormone and prolactin. This happens in order to mobilize energy to help us adapt to new circumstances.

Oxytocin induces anti-stress-like effects, such as reduction of blood pressure and cortisol levels. It increases the pain threshold, exerts an anxiolytic-like effect and stimulates various types of positive social interactions. In addition, it promotes growth and healing.

Adrenaline, cortisol and norepinephrine are the three major stress hormones.

Adrenaline

Known as the 'fight or flight' hormone, it is produced by the adrenal glands when it receives a message from the brain that a stressful situation has presented itself.

What it does: Adrenaline, along with norepinephrine, is largely responsible for the immediate reaction that we feel when stressed. It increases the heart rate and gives us a sudden surge of energy needed to run away from a dangerous situation. Adrenaline surge also helps us keep our attention focused on the threat.

Norepinephrine

A hormone similar to adrenaline that is released from the adrenal glands as well as in the brain.

What it does: The primary role of norepinephrine, like adrenaline, is arousal.

Cortisol

A steroid hormone, commonly known as stress hormone, is produced by the adrenal glands.

What it does: Comparatively, it takes more time for us to feel the effect of cortisol when we face stress. The release of this hormone is a multi-step process involving two additional minor hormones.

First, the amygdala recognizes the threat. It sends a message to the part of the brain called the hypothalamus that releases corticotropin-releasing hormone (CRH). CRH then signals the pituitary gland to release the adrenocorticotropic hormone, which in turn triggers the adrenal glands to produce cortisol.

During survival mode, the required optimal amount of cortisol can be lifesaving. It helps to maintain fluid balance and blood pressure and regulates certain body functions that are not crucial at the moment, such as reproductive drive, immunity, digestion and growth.

When faced with a problem, the body continuously releases cortisol. Excessive cortisol can suppress the immune system, increase blood pressure and sugar, decrease libido, produce acne, contribute to obesity and more. In addition to these three major hormones, oestrogen and testosterone also affect how we react to stress, so do the neurotransmitters dopamine and serotonin.

Nutrition and Balanced Healthy Diet

It is necessary to consume healthy, balanced food that offers all the essential nutrients for our body to maintain the energy balance. We are very conscious about using good quality engine oil in our vehicles to make sure that it runs efficiently. However, we are hardly bothered about the quality and nutritious value of the food we consume, which is important for the effective functioning of our body and brain.

According to research conducted by Julia Rucklidge, a clinical psychologist, there is a direct correlation between the quality of food intake and mental health. The risk that we all face is that we tend to choose food on the basis of visual appeal and taste rather than on common sense and reasoning. The more we drift away from healthy food, the more challenges we pose for ourselves.

Our senses are hijacked by the taste and smell of food. In fact, food is one of the major addictions for many. This addiction does not receive as much attention as alcoholism or drugs. It is important to stop reaching out for factory-made food products and to start developing a taste for natural, healthy food. The thumb rule is that foods closer to their natural form are healthier than processed food products.

Sound/Adequate Sleep

There is a strong relationship between good sleep and emotional well-being. Sleep deprivation impacts the psychological state and mental health as well. Good sleep builds emotional resilience. The lack of sleep promotes negative thinking, and we become emotionally vulnerable. Some of the major factors that prevent sound sleep are anxiety, fear and depression.

Neuroimaging and neurochemistry have indicated the impact of inadequate sleep on both emotional resilience and mental health. The lack of sound sleep has been identified as one of the significant reasons for mental depression. The other impact of inadequate or disturbed sleep is anxiety disorder, which further leads to restlessness.

The hypothalamic–pituitary–adrenal (HPA) axis regulates sleep in humans. Sleeplessness occurs when the HPA axis is very low. The presence of cortisol keeps us awake, depriving us of much-needed sleep. Disturbance in sleep is thus associated with elevated cortisol levels and HPS dysfunction. Quality of sleep directly influences our emotions.

To help our bodies run efficiently, it is important to give attention to all the aforementioned aspects. It is necessary to choose the right kinds of fuel to function optimally, both physically and mentally.

Emotional Fuel Checklist

The following questions would help you in estimating the 'energy balance' to fuel EI.

Put a tick (✓) mark if you completely agree to the statement or else a cross (✗) mark.

	EI Fuel Exercise	Tick
	Adequate Sleep	
1	I have sound and timely sleep of minimum 6 to 7 hours everyday.	
2	I have uninterrupted deep sleep.	
3	I sleep without any medication.	
4	I feel fresh after my sleep.	
	Mental GYM/Meditation	
1	I do meditation (breathing exercise/Yoga) atleast four times a week.	
2	I feel recharged after meditation.	
3	I pray for 15-20 minutes at least four times a week.	
4	I spend time with nature a few times a week.	
	Sports, Physical Activity	
1	I engage in sports or physical activity atleast four times a week.	
2	I feel good about my physical condition.	
3	I enjoy physical activities.	
4	I experience a better frame of mind due to the physical activity.	
	Food and Nutrition	
1	I eat when I am hungry at regular intervals.	
2	I eat balanced and nutritious food.	
3	I avoid oily and fried food.	
4	I can say no to food when its unhealthy or when I am full.	

Compliment yourself for statements which are marked (✓).

Introspect and develop an action plan on the basis of the rest of the statements.

My 'Wheel of Life' Activity

Step 1 (A Day in My Life)

Write down various tasks and activities you perform in a typical day of your life on the basis of the last 12 months.

_____	_____
_____	_____
_____	_____
_____	_____
_____	_____
_____	_____
_____	_____
_____	_____
_____	_____
_____	_____
_____	_____

Step 2

On the basis of 'A Day in My Life' suggested earlier, plot 'my wheel of life'. Consider the wheel as a typical day or a week. Plot the size of the angle on the basis of the time spent on the activity in a typical day or week.

My Wheel of Life

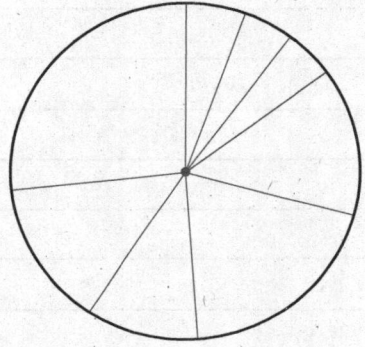

Step 3

Now, look at the EI fuel balance. How much EI fuel do you generate and consume? Remember that adequate sleep, mental gym/meditation, physical activity and balanced food and nutrition are the aspects that generate this fuel. The rest of the activities just burn EI fuel. Summarize the emotional fuel balance you have on a given day.

My EI Fuel Balance: Action Plan

List down the key actions that you would initiate to convert your EI fuel balance.

_____

_____

_____

_____

_____

_____

_____

_____

_____

_____

_____

_____

_____

_____

_____

Step 4: Exchange

Exchange your thoughts and experiences with people you trust on the basis of your 'EI fuel balance'.

Discuss the following questions:

- In which of the activities do I gain EI fuel?
- Which are the activities that burn my EI fuel?
- What are the specific actions that I must take to change the balance to more positive?
- What are the activities I must preserve or further strengthen?

Compassion

The third way to build EI is to be compassionate towards others. An interesting study conducted by social psychologists John Darley and C. Daniel Batson on 'Being a Good Samaritan, Psychology of Helping' researched the behaviour of helping others.

The objective was to find out whether religious thoughts have any influence on making people feel a strong need to help others. This is based on the common belief that religious thoughts inspire people to be compassionate. At the same time, they wanted to find out if 'time pressure' had anything to do with the impulse to help.

Students were divided into two groups. One group was given topics related to 'vocational careers' and the other group of students was given the topic of 'being a good Samaritan'. They were asked to prepare a brief talk on the subject.

Students were separated and were given a different 'sense of urgency'. One group was informed that there was 'no hurry' and the other group was told that it was rather urgent, with stiff timelines. They staged people appearing to be in pain and distress in the vicinity of the students. The finding was very interesting.

Students with the topic 'vocational careers' were prone to helping others more, as they were the group with comparatively more liberal time to prepare. The group that was working on the topic of 'being a good Samaritan' was less prone to be helpful. It was contrary to the behaviour indicated by the topic they were preparing.

The study concluded that students who were in a hurry due to stiff timelines were less inclined to be compassionate. In today's world, we are all running towards deadlines and hence perpetually in a hurry. This makes us less prone to being compassionate.

Hurrying Prevents Helping

Hurrying all the time is a predicament that we face in our lives. We have created a life packed with tight schedules, leaving hardly any time to show compassion. It is time we manage the pace of our lives and minimize this mindless rush.

According to research done in the field of neuroscience, our default mode is to help others spontaneously, especially those in distress situations. We automatically identify and empathize with others due to the presence of 'mirror neurons'. The reason for the lower level of compassion and insensitivity that we display could be due to our predisposition with 'self'. Even if we choose to help others, it is most likely for feeling good about ourselves rather than to make them happy.

True compassion is about putting 'others' before 'self'. The common behaviour observed in the world today leans towards individualism. Compassion can be contagious, as the act of compassion can trigger a similar emotion in other people around us.

Compassion is triggered by empathy. It is an important mechanism that helps to build EI. At times, we might not be able to explain compassion, but all of us can recognize this emotion when we experience it. On the other hand, recognizing a lack of compassion is much easier.

Cole-King and Gilbert defined compassion as being 'sensitive to the distress and pain of others, with a commitment to try to do something about it'. Compassion demands action from us. Just feeling for somebody in suffering can be pity or sympathy, but compassion is a higher level of emotion.

Acts of kindness release endorphins and oxytocin, creating new connections in our neurons in the posterior superior temporal cortex of the brain. Repeated acts of compassion tend to become a habit and is eventually exercised more naturally. Even when we witness, imagine or visualize compassion, a similar effect can be observed in the brain.

There is an important link between compassion and healing process. Studies among health professionals indicate a strong connection between their workload and compassion they display towards patients. The main reason for this is compassion fatigue.

Compassion Attributes

Necessary attributes that help us act with compassion include distress tolerance, non-judgement, sensitivity and interest. When all four attributes come together, the chances of being compassionate is enhanced.

Attributes of Compassion

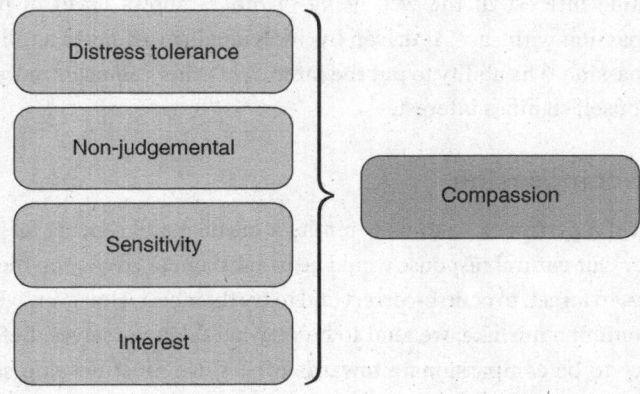

Distress Tolerance

It is the ability to withstand difficult situations and the willingness to face them. No individual enjoys distress, but their willingness to face encumbrances and to take the trouble to help others signifies distress tolerance.

Non-judgemental

The ability to see a person in distress without any preconceived notion, biases and historical background makes us non-judgemental. Without this ability, we might not be able to move towards compassion.

Sensitivity

Sensitivity indicates the strength of our emotional antennae. The ability to see pain and suffering in others, even when not expressed. If we lack empathy, our sensitivity towards others is likely to be lower.

Interest

Genuine interest in the well-being of others allows us to display compassion with ease. If driven by 'individualism', it takes a toll on compassion. The ability to put the interest of others equal or more to that of self signifies interest.

Self-compassion

What if a person close to us commits a mistake and repents for the same? Our natural response would be to ask them to go easy on themselves, to forget, to course-correct and to try their best. However, when we commit a mistake, we tend to be very harsh on ourselves. Before we try to be compassionate towards others, we must develop self-compassion. Unless we learn how to forgive and go easy on ourselves for mistakes or wrong decisions, we may fall prey to self-critical mode. Self-compassion needs to precede compassion towards others.

Success Factors

The definition of success differs from person to person. Generally, the understanding of success is lopsided, either tilted towards financial success or social status and recognition. Social media has deeply driven the idea that being successful is all about online presence and getting lots of 'likes' and 'comments' for our posts and displaying financial opulence.

Success can be achieved when we work towards progress in the following five dimensions.

Five Dimensions of Success

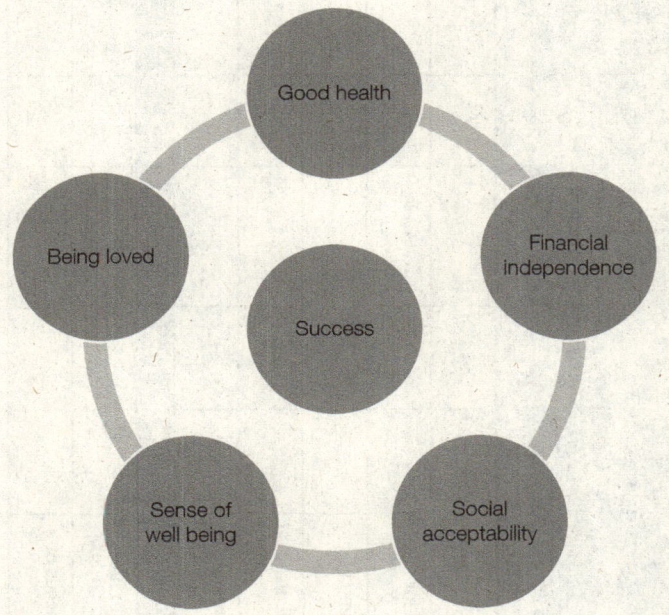

We tend to pursue some of these dimensions and ignore the rest. Our education system offers multiple subjects. When we perform well in all subjects, we score a distinction. Similarly, we can gain the distinction of being successful in life when we perform well in all these five dimensions. Disproportionate investment of time and energy in one dimension leads to ineffectiveness. EI helps us to achieve success in all five dimensions.

EI fuels all the components of success in a composite manner. It would not be incorrect to say that the way in which we manage and regulate our emotions, motivate ourselves, display empathy and demonstrate social skills leads to success in our lives. The following table helps us measure our standing on the success scale.

S. No.	Self-check–Success Factor	Mark in Scale of 1-5				
	Statements	Do not agree	Maybe	Somewhat agree	Agree	Strongly agree
		1	2	3	4	5
Health						
1	I am devoid of any long enduring diseases such as diabetes, blood pressure and heart ailment.					
2	I am fit to perform all physical activities needed for leading a normal life.					
3	I do not get physically drained and tired by the end of the day.					
4	I have the flexibility in my body to perform my daily activities.					
5	My body functions such as digestion, bowel movements function normally.					
Financial						
1	I have adequate financial resources to take care of me and my dependents needs currently.					
2	I have financial planning to take care of future needs of my family.					

#	Statement					
3	I have adequate financial resources to take care in case of no employment for 6 months.					
4	I have made arrangements to take care of the medical expenses of my family.					
5	I have made arrangements for taking care of my post-retirement financial needs.					

Social acceptance and recognition

#	Statement					
1	I am needed and loved by my family.					
2	I am contributing well profesionally.					
3	I am involved in social gatherings.					
4	I have received formal social recognition.					
5	I am sought for advice by others.					

Sense of wellbeing

#	Statement					
1	I do not experience stress frequently.					
2	I enjoy whatever I am doing at personal and professional level.					
3	I am able to smile and laugh frequently.					
4	I think positive and I am optimistic.					
5	I enjoy the current moments of life.					

(Continued)

(Continued)

	Self-check–Success factor	Mark in Scale of 1-5				
		Do not agree	May be	Somewhat agree	Agree	Strongly agree
S No	Statements	1	2	3	4	5
Being loved						
1	My near and dear ones express their love to me.					
2	I express love to my near and dear ones.					
3	I am missed when not present with my near and dear ones.					
4	I feel wanted by near and dear ones.					
5	I miss my near and dear ones when away.					

- A score of less than 100 indicates that there is scope for development.
- Evaluate all statements in which you scored less than 4. Introspect how you can develop on them.

Driving EI

After building EI, it is time to learn how to drive EI. The following steps will help drive us towards an emotionally intelligent personal and professional lives.

The development of mindfulness, resilience and compassion helps to 'build EI'. Driving EI is about implementing EI while dealing with real-life situations and people. In order to gain a common understanding of the steps that help us drive EI, here is an analogy of driving a car. Brake, mirrors, gears, rules and steer help us navigate through the traffic. Similarly, driving EI helps us navigate through difficult and challenging life situations.

These steps are sequential and need to be practised, especially when faced with challenging situations and people. The more we work towards perfecting these steps, the more would EI manifest effortlessly. At times, we might tend to ignore these steps, driven by our emotional impulses. The steps are illustrated in a simple manner to help us remember and implement them. Enjoy a pleasurable drive towards an emotionally intelligent life.

 **Brake**

Pause to Realize Stress and Reduce It

When faced with emotionally charged situations, as discussed earlier, our amygdala hijacks our responses. It limits our ability to think rationally, as blood circulation to the cortex region is cut off and reptilian emotional brain takes over. When stress levels are high, it leads to overbearing behaviour, with little or no control over our actions. Survival instincts are at play, and we act devoid of reasoning.

At this stage, we need to apply the 'brake' and let emotions subside, not allowing them to take over our responses. 'Brake' is about taking a pause and giving ourselves the opportunity to recognize our

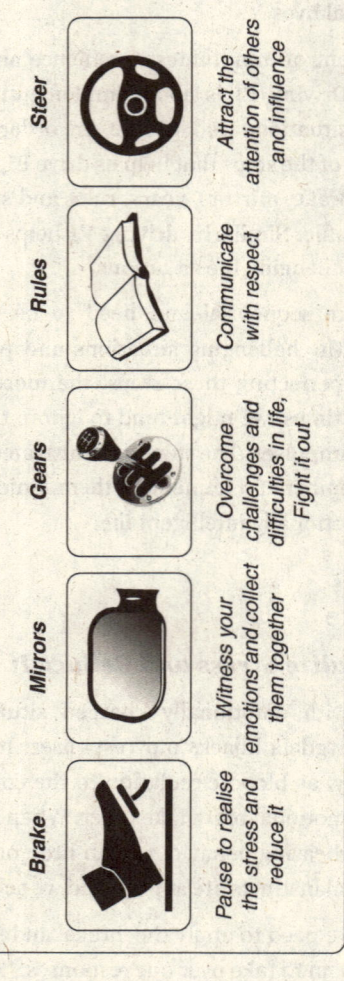

Driving EI

Brake — Pause to realise the stress and reduce it

Mirrors — Witness your emotions and collect them together

Gears — Overcome challenges and difficulties in life, Fight it out

Rules — Communicate with respect

Steer — Attract the attention of others and influence

emotions. It is for providing us with space to enable self-awareness to dwell upon us. It is the first step towards reducing our stress levels. If we do not apply the 'brake', we are likely to drive around rashly with our emotions.

Reduce the speed to think with clarity. This is important for avoiding emotional hijack. We must learn how to apply the brake on our impulsive reactive behaviour. If we are unable to apply the brake and manage our emotions, there is no harm in seeking help.

Recall Your 'Amygdala Rescue Mantra'

One of the methods to quickly apply the brake is to use the 'amygdala rescue mantra'. Recall the 'amygdala rescue mantra' developed in the earlier part of the book. Write down the mantra drafted by you.

_____

_____

_____

_____

The mantra will help create awareness, apply the 'brake' and escape from the amygdala hijack. Repeat the mantra several times when faced with a difficult situation. With the repeated chanting of the mantra in our minds, we can successfully apply the 'brake' to our emotions.

Brake and Release Activity

Try this 2-minute exercise to obtain relief from stress. This exercise can be done anywhere, at your workplace, while travelling or at home. This is an instant quick fix exercise that will help you overcome the amygdala hijack. It helps create a time-space for us to enable us to choose a more effective response after moving away from the grip of emotional hijack.

The method is simple and can be done in a sitting, standing or lying down position. The process is to tighten the muscles in different parts of the body and release them after a span of five seconds. Start the tightening process from the feet and move upwards to the face.

Do the tightening and relaxing of your muscles for five seconds. Take a deep breath as you tighten the muscles and gradually breathe out as you release the tension.

You may follow these steps:

1. Tighten the muscles in your feet and hands and release.
2. Tighten your calf and thigh muscles and let it go by releasing the tension.
3. Tighten your pelvic region and back muscles and release.
4. Do the same with your stomach muscles.
5. Finally do the same with the facial muscles.

Repeat the exercise for at least 2 minutes.

As you release the tension from the muscles, try to experience the sensation on your skin, muscles and bones. When faced with a stressful situation, this exercise offers quick relief, bringing down our stress levels. It helps us escape from the clasp of our amygdala.

The Case of Road Rage

I was travelling with my colleague on the express highway between Mumbai and Pune. Midway through the journey, a car travelling at a high speed cut across the lane and overtook our car within a margin of fewer than 2 feet. This shocked my colleague who was behind the wheels. The shock soon turned into anger, and he stepped on the accelerator pedal to catch up with the car that overtook us rashly. Within a few seconds, he reduced the speed of the car and said, 'it is not worth it. We do not need to endanger our lives to teach someone a lesson.' He calmed down immediately, and we were back to our normal conversation.

If my colleague had not applied the 'brakes' on his emotional hijack, it could have ended in a road rage incident. He further added, 'at times in life, we need to know where, on whom and for what issue should we dispense our emotions. A few years back, I would not have been able to control my anger. I have learnt my lesson the hard way,' he concluded. This is an example of applying 'brakes' on our emotions as we drive EI.

 **Look into Mirrors**

Witness Your Emotions and Collect Them Together

Emotions serve as the primary driver for communication. It is important to look at ourselves and recognize emotions that we and others around us are experiencing. This is similar to the method of driving a car, where we take a good look at the rear and front mirrors before making a move.

Emotions are very essential. If the emotional part of the brain is removed, we would lose motivation and the desire to do anything. Emotions need to be used and managed effectively. Many fail to implement the 'looking in the mirror' part, drifting away with the flow of emotions rather than taking stock of them and channelizing them in the right direction.

If we drive the car without looking in the mirrors, it would be dangerous and could lead to accidents. Similarly, if we do not understand the emotions of self and others, it can lead to accidents in human interactions. Self-regulation is the process that helps in managing our emotions. This is the most challenging part of driving EI.

Emotional awareness, at every moment, is important. Core emotions such as anger, sadness, fear and joy are experienced by us each day of our lives. These emotions cannot be avoided, but we can be well aware of and conscious of them and exercise appropriate choices. To be conscious of emotions is also about being aware of emotions experienced by others.

A Case of Emotional Diary

A close friend of mine, a senior manager of a large corporation, had strained relationships with people. He was highly result-oriented and pushed his subordinates to get things done. He was demanding and aggressive while dealing with them and often expressed anger in the form of emotional outbursts. He used to get things done but landed up messing up his relationships.

When this behaviour started affecting his family life, it was a wake-up call. As he introspected, he could not pinpoint the trigger for his emotional outbursts. He chose to maintain an 'emotional diary' to course-correct himself. He started documenting his emotional outbursts and the cause for the same. He also noted the impact of his behaviour on others. He gradually started becoming aware of his emotions, thereby managing his responses better.

 Change Gears

Overcome Challenges and Difficulties in Life, Fight It Out

Life is bound to bring forth many challenging situations. The way we deal with them and overcome them determines our overall effectiveness. No one can escape challenges. What we can do is learn how to 'change gears' as we face them. Just like we need to change gears in the car on the basis of the gradient in the road while driving, it is important to rightly use self-motivation and momentum to manage challenging life situations.

Playfulness, smile and humour help in managing challenges. They are tools that enable us to relax and calm our nerves while facing difficulties. If we are tense, mournful and of a serious disposition, we quickly sink into despair.

Maintaining a positive frame of mind helps us manage difficult situations and prevent us from being imprisoned by negative emotions. The ability to visualize the final outcome with a sense of purpose will help us overcome the challenges with ease. Mastering the art of changing emotional gears helps us get through difficult times, to maintain our relationships, to be creative and to drive seamlessly towards achievements.

Changing gears also involves talking to our 'alter ego', our alternative self. We need to use positive and constructive language when we talk to ourselves. This activates our internal locus of control and cuts out negative influences from the environment. If we succumb to negative and counterproductive thoughts, we risk losing the verve needed to change gears and surmount challenging situations. Humour and shared joy minimize the impact of negative emotions prevailing upon us. It helps us to reduce our stress levels and focus on our achievement orientation.

A Case of Rebuilding Career

The general manager of a print media company known to me, heading the sales function for the western region, was summoned by the management. He was asked to resign as the organization was facing financial strain. The company was looking at managing the business with a lesser number of people. He was offered the option of operating as a dealer for the company at variable cost. He gracefully accepted the offer, as he did not have any other option at that point of time. He operated as a dealer for nearly a year and did moderately well. He had to face the uphill task of canvassing for a product, which had a declining demand in the market due to alternative online solutions available to customers. Consequently, he went through financial strain on the personal front. He had to strive to provide for two grown-up daughters and a spouse who chose not to work, preferring to focus on the family. He was the sole breadwinner with huge liabilities, in business and loans.

Meanwhile, he started working on an alternative business idea, which was related to learning and development. He always had a passion for this profession. In a few years, he was immensely successful in the field of learning and development. In a decade, he was a name to reckon with in his chosen field. The consulting firm set up by him brought him financial gains and recognition that he could never have dreamt of if he had continued in employment. He never complained or had negative feelings about the decision taken by his company. On the contrary, he was thankful for the decision to lay him off, as it helped him move out of his comfort zone and achieve greater success. He changed gears in order to manage difficult situations, always carried a positive attitude devoid of malice or negativity. He was not distracted by negative thoughts from the environment. He established a consultancy firm, just kept changing gears seamlessly, thereby achieving immense success, in the true sense as referred earlier in the book.

 **Respect Rules**

Communicate with Respect

When we interact with people, conflicts and differences are bound to occur. It is important that we follow the rules of effective human interaction with the help of our tone, body language and choice of words. The differences, if addressed in a respectful way, go a long way in building strong relationships.

Empathy for people enables us to realize their perspective. When we do not perceive conflicts and differences of opinion as threats, we tend to act with more creativity, trust and mutual respect. Just like the way we need to follow the traffic rules while we drive our cars, we have to respect the rules of effective human interaction.

When in conflict, it is easy to resort to criticism, contempt and defensiveness, which inevitably leads to a toxic relationship. It is necessary to follow the rules and to communicate assertively without hurting the sentiments of others. It is possible to strike a balance between communicating what we want and be respectful at the same time.

Listening occupies a significant space in the human interaction rule book. Most of the differences can be resolved if we listen with the intent of understanding. Fear of losing, preconceived notions, past experiences and ignorance prevents us from actually listening to others.

Managing conflicts can make or mar relationships. The rules of body language, tone of voice and choice of words need to be abided by, even under the most challenging situations. The ability to prevent our emotions from taking over our vocabulary and body language separate emotionally intelligent people from the rest. Despite best intentions, not abiding by the rules of effective and conducive communication can result in broken relationships. Hence, always play by the rules. It is definitely possible to communicate hard-hitting facts wrapped in the velvet gloves of diplomacy and humour.

Case of Mr Cool

The CEO of an organization was faced with the dilemma of rationalizing the workforce during the slowdown. He had to let go of hundreds of people across various functions. He called upon the HR manager and insisted on setting up a meeting with the team members being given the pink slip, against the advice of the HR head.

He assembled all of them in the town hall and allowed them to ask questions. He received a lot of angry brickbats due to the decision. He was questioned on the criteria and was hounded with challenging questions such as 'why me' and 'why were we not informed earlier'. He understood that the team members were reacting due to their anger and disappointment. He listened to each question calmly without losing his cool and explained the process, the criteria and what the future holds for them. The session went on almost for two hours and not once was he out of control, despite some personal verbal attacks on him. His communication was clear, firm, yet polite. At the end of the session, many members came up to him, appreciated him for organizing the meeting, commended him for the manner in which he conducted himself with dignity and respect for others. He did live by the rules, despite the challenging situation.

 **Power Steer**

Attract Attention of Others and Influence

Once we learn to 'brake', 'look into the mirror', 'change gears' and 'respect rules', we naturally tend to attract people around us. Driving EI will enable us to influence people. No one likes to deal with people who are not in control of their emotions. If our behaviour is unpredictable, the people around us would maintain a safe distance from us. The power of influencing people thus stems from the effective display of EI.

We can power steer our way through people and build effective relationships with them. Leadership is all about influencing thoughts and actions of people. Investment in learning how to drive EI will help us become a successful leader.

Steer through challenging situations without being abrasive. When we practise brake, mirrors, gears and rules, we will be able to steer through the most difficult situations. We will gain the skill to drive with EI, navigating effortlessly through the tough terrains of life. Steering is not just confined to challenging situations but also extends to building effective relationships.

Mapping, Building and Driving EI

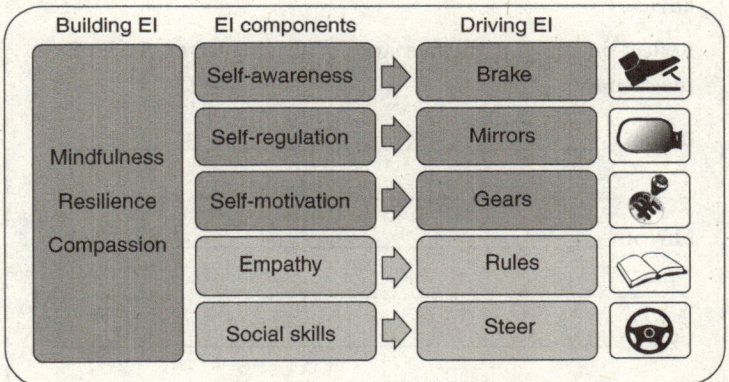

r -

Driving EI Activity

Your teenage son is adamant on choosing a career in dramatics. You are of the opinion that he has made this choice because he is not good at academics and is trying to find an easy way out. You have tried to explain your point of view on several occasions in the past, but your son is very persistent in opting for the career of his choice.

Your son further expresses that he loves the creative field and wishes to take up a career in film-making after a few years of experience in dramatics. He is not keen on pursuing his postgraduation in science and technology, as this is not related to his area of interest. He pleads with you to spend the money saved for his education on the dramatics course.

Your son approaches you to seek your permission to apply for the course he wishes to pursue. You are very worried about his future and also angry that he is not willing to listen to your advice.

Reflect on applying the five steps of 'driving EI' on the basis of the scenario.

Brake: _____

_____

Mirrors: _____

_____

Gears: _____

_____

Rules: _____

_____

Steer: _____

_____

Key tips for driving EI

Brake

I shall take a pause.
I shall calm down my emotions.

Look into the mirror

I shall try to understand the emotions that I am experiencing.
I shall try to understand the emotions experienced by others.

I shall collect my thoughts.
I shall choose to respond and not be driven by my emotions.

Change gears
I shall face the challenge posed.
I shall not give up easily.
I shall try my very best to overcome the challenges.
I shall use humour and playfulness appropriately to ease my nerves.

Respect rules
I shall be careful in my choice of words.
I shall use positive body language.
I shall not fall prey to negative emotions.

Power steer
I shall try my best to influence people.
I shall maintain relationships with people.
I shall be a role model in managing emotions.

Salient Points

- Driving EI involves using the emotional fuel and drive, following the steps of 'brake', 'look into mirrors' and 'change gears' and steer to successfully navigate through challenging life situations.
- *Brake:* Brake helps us pause and witness the stress caused by the situation and consciously reduce it.
- *Mirrors:* Mirrors help us witness the emotions we are experiencing and collect them together.

- *Gears:* Gears help us to shift perspective and approach, whenever necessary, to overcome challenges and difficulties in life.
- *Rules:* Following the rules of EI helps us to communicate with respect and dignity.
- *Steer:* Steering is about being persuasive and influencing, thereby attracting people.

EI Strength Finder Tool

Please take the opportunity to conduct a self-assessment of EI.
It would provide you the opportunity to develop areas of your EI.

EMOTIONAL INTELLIGENCE- STRENGTH FINDER
General principles for working with the tool
1. No one in the world can help you, if you refuse to help yourself
2. If you are not honest with your responses, the result of this questionnaire will refuse to speak the truth to you
3. Kindly introspect and respond realistically, not Idealistically
4. This is a tool for development; hence it would help you only if you respond truthfully
Guidelines for the tool
1. This is not a test but rather a Self-Assessment tool
2. The time available to respond to the statements in the tool is 10 Minutes
3. Follow your instinctive "Top of the mind" response
4. Respond to the statements serially starting from 1 to 50
5. Do not spend too much time on any statement
6. Do not revisit any response after you have made your choices
Instructions
Assess and score each of the statements in the questionnaire
Score your assessment, using the following scale that indicates:
1: Does NOT apply at all
2: Applies SOMETIMES
3: Applies about HALF the time
4: Applies MOST of the times
5: ALWAYS applies to you

No.	Statements	Please circle the number applicable to you				
1	I realize when I am angry	1	2	3	4	5
2	I can bounce back from bad mood easily	1	2	3	4	5
3	I prefer to encourage myself during challenging tasks	1	2	3	4	5
4	I can understand other's point of view with ease	1	2	3	4	5
5	I connect with people well	1	2	3	4	5
6	I can understand the emotion being experienced by me	1	2	3	4	5
7	I manage my impulses well	1	2	3	4	5
8	I can manage my priorities well	1	2	3	4	5
9	I am judgmental when understanding people	1	2	3	4	5
10	I can influence people	1	2	3	4	5
11	I realize that I am undergoing stress	1	2	3	4	5
12	I can overcome negative thoughts	1	2	3	4	5
13	I complete tasks on time	1	2	3	4	5
14	I can imagine the feelings of others	1	2	3	4	5
15	I get along with people comfortably	1	2	3	4	5
16	I realize when I am disturbed	1	2	3	4	5
17	I maintain my cool while dealing with people	1	2	3	4	5
18	I take lead in starting new things	1	2	3	4	5
19	I can feel the pain faced by others	1	2	3	4	5
20	I prefer to work with various teams	1	2	3	4	5
21	I realise, when I am tensed	1	2	3	4	5
22	I keep calm in conflict situations	1	2	3	4	5
23	I go after my goals, once they are set	1	2	3	4	5

No.	Statements	Please circle the number applicable to you				
24	I can sense the moods of other	1	2	3	4	5
25	I adapt to changes comfortably	1	2	3	4	5
26	I realize when I am being unreasonable with others	1	2	3	4	5
27	I can change my mood quickly if I wish to	1	2	3	4	5
28	I tend to love what I do	1	2	3	4	5
29	I see that people are different, when faced with conflict	1	2	3	4	5
30	I understand the dynamics of a group well	1	2	3	4	5
31	I am aware of the emotions I experience	1	2	3	4	5
32	I leave behind my professional stress when I go home	1	2	3	4	5
33	I wait patiently to get the results for the work done by me	1	2	3	4	5
34	I realize, when I hurt others	1	2	3	4	5
35	I am keen that others should be happy in my company	1	2	3	4	5
36	I understand when my words and actions impact others	1	2	3	4	5
37	I am calm and cool about life	1	2	3	4	5
38	I complete work as per plan	1	2	3	4	5
39	I know when people around me are disturbed	1	2	3	4	5
40	I like to work in teams and build a relationship	1	2	3	4	5
41	I am aware when I am tired	1	2	3	4	5
42	I can avoid distractions and focus on the goal	1	2	3	4	5

(Continued)

No.	Statements	Please circle the number applicable to you				
43	I can bounce back quickly, when I feel low	1	2	3	4	5
44	I can feel the pain of others easily even when not expressed	1	2	3	4	5
45	I am good at resolving conflicts among people	1	2	3	4	5
46	I can understand my state of mind while dealing with people	1	2	3	4	5
47	I can postpone expressing my feelings and opinions	1	2	3	4	5
48	I do better when my inner voice pushes me	1	2	3	4	5
49	I understand the feelings when others disagree with me	1	2	3	4	5
50	I can communicate well to the understanding of others	1	2	3	4	5

EI Strength Finder Scoring

Record your 1 to 5 scores for the questionnaire statements in the grid below. The grid organizes the statements into emotional competency lists.

Self-awareness (SA)	Self-regulation (SR)	Self-motivation (SM)	Empathy (EM)	Social skills (SS)
1	2	3	4	5
6	7	8	9	10
11	12	13	14	15
16	17	18	19	20
21	22	23	24	25
26	27	28	29	30
31	32	33	34	35
36	37	38	39	40
41	42	43	44	45
46	47	48	49	50
Total SA	SR	SM	EM	SS

Scores <45 has an increasing scale of scope for development

(Continued)

(Continued)

EI component	Strengths	Needs attention	Developmental priority
Self-awareness			
Self-regulation			
Self-motivation			
Empathy			
Social skills			

Suggested Readings

Ballatt, J., and P. Campling. 2011. 'Building the Case for Kindness'. In *Intelligent Kindness: Reforming the Culture of Healthcare*, 33–47. London: Royal College of Psychiatrists.

Benson, Herbert, and Miriam Z. Klipper. 1974. *The Relaxation Response*. New York, NY: Avon Books.

Cherniss, Cary. 1999. 'The Business Case for Emotional Intelligence'. Prepared for the *Consortium for Research on Emotional Intelligence*. Middlesex County, NJ: Rutgers University. Available at http://www.eiconsortium.org/pdf/business_case_for_ei.pdf (accessed on 27 November 2020).

Chopra, Deepak. 1994. *The Seven Spiritual Laws of Success*. Novato, CA: New World Library.

Dalai Lama, Desmond Tutu, and Douglas Carlton Abrams. 2016. *The Book of Joy*. London: Hutchinson.

David, Susan. 2019. 'A Vocabulary of Your Emotions'. In *Everyday Emotional Intelligence*. Boston, MA: Harvard Business Review Press.

Eurich, Tasha. 2018. *What Self-Awareness Really Is (and How to Cultivate It)*. Brighton, MA: Harvard Business Review Press.

Goleman, Daniel. 2000. *Working with Emotional Intelligence*. New York, NY: Bantam.

Goleman, Daniel, Annie McKee, and Shawn Achor. 2018. *Everyday Emotional Intelligence*. Brighton, MA: Harvard Business School Publishing Corporation.

Harvard Business Review, Daniel Goleman, Richard Boyatzis, Annie McKee, and Sydney Finkelstein. 2015. *HBR's 10 Must Reads on Emotional Intelligence*. Brighton, MA: Harvard Business School Publishing Corporation.

Harvard Business Review, Daniel Gilbert, Annie McKee, Gretchen Spreitzer and Teresa M. Amabile. 2017. *Emotional Intelligence Happiness*. Boston, MA: Harvard Business Review Press.

Harvard Business Review, Daniel Goleman, Robert Steven Kaplan, Susan David, and Tasha Eurich. 2017. *Self-Awareness (HBR Emotional Intelligence Series)*. Brighton, MA: Harvard Business School Publishing Corporation.

Harvard Business Review, Daniel Goleman, Ellen Langer, Susan David, and Christina Congleton. 2017. *Mindfulness (HBR Emotional Intelligence Series)*. Brighton, MA: Harvard Business Review Press.

Harvard Business Review, Diane Coutu, Daniel Goleman, David Kopans, Sheila Heen, Douglas Stone, Jeffrey A. Sonnenfeld, Andrew J. Ward, Shawn Achor and Michelle Gielan. 2017. *Resilience and Emotional Intelligence (HBR Emotional Intelligence Series)*. Boston, MA: Harvard Business Review Press.

Helliwell, John F., Richard Layard, Jeffrey D. Sachs, and Jan-Emmanuel De Neve. 2020. *World Happiness Report*. Available at https://worldhappiness.report/ed/2020/ (accessed on 27 November 2020).

Jain, Neera. 2011. 'In Quest of Enhanced EQ'. In *Emotional Intelligence & Leadership*, edited by Shamira Soren Malekar. Mumbai: Forum for Emotional Intelligence Learning, Excel Books.

Kapadia, Mala. 2011. 'Emotional Intelligence, Gen X and Y and Quarter Life Crisis'. In *Emotional Intelligence & Leadership*, edited by Shamira Soren Malekar. Mumbai: Forum for Emotional Intelligence Learning, Excel Books.

Krznaric, Roman. 2014. *Empathy: Why It Matters, and How to Get It*. Toronto: Kobo.

Malekar, Shamira, and Ishani Doshi. 2011. 'Social Relationships A Study'. In *Emotional Intelligence & Leadership*, edited by Shamira Soren Malekar. Mumbai: Forum for Emotional Intelligence Learning, Excel Books.

Reyers, Anne. 2007. 'Emotional Regulation at Walt Disney World Deep Acting Vs. Surface Acting'. Tampa, FL: University of Tampa. Available at https://stars.library.ucf.edu/cgi/viewcontent.cgi?referer=&httpsredir=1&article=2954&context=etd (accessed on 27 November 2020).

Salehi, Mahdi, Mohammadreza Zadeh, Alireza Ghaderi and Alaleh Tabasi. 2016. 'A Study of the Effect of Education and Academic Environment on Emotional Intelligence on Accounting Students in Iran'. International Education Studies 9 (1). Available at http://www.ccsenet.org/journal/index.php/ies/article/view/56006 (accessed on 19 January 2021).

Sen, Anjana. 2011. 'Effect of Meditation on the Brain with Implications for Emotional Intelligence'. In *Emotional Intelligence & Leadership*, edited by Shamira Soren Malekar. Mumbai: Forum for Emotional Intelligence Learning, Excel Books.

Singh, Dalip. 2010. *Emotional Intelligence at Work*. New Delhi: SAGE Publications.

Singh, S. B., and V. K. Gupta. 2011. 'Parenting with Emotional Intelligence'. In *Emotional Intelligence & Leadership*, edited by Shamira Soren Malekar. Mumbai: Forum for Emotional Intelligence Learning, Excel Books.

Sterrett, Emily A. 2000. *The Manager's Pocket Guide to Emotional Intelligence*. Amherst, MA: HRD Press.

Vohs, Kathleen D. and Roy F. Baumeister, eds. 2011. *Handbook of Self-Regulation Research, Theory, and Applications*. New York, NY: The Guilford Press.

Watson, Richard. 2010. *Future Files*. Nicholas Brealey Publishing.

———— 2017. *Emotional Happiness*. Brighton, MA: Harvard Business Review Press.

Scan QR code to access the
Penguin Random House India website